VILMUNDAR SAGA VIÐUTAN

THE SAGA OF VILMUNDUR THE OUTSIDER

EDITED AND TRANSLATED BY
JONATHAN Y. H. HUI

VIKING SOCIETY FOR NORTHERN RESEARCH
UNIVERSITY COLLEGE LONDON
2021

VIKING SOCIETY TEXTS

General Editors
Alison Finlay
Carl Phelpstead

© Viking Society for Northern Research 2021
Printed by Short Run Press Limited, Exeter

ISBN: 978-1-914070-00-6

Cover image: A full-page illustration of Vilmundur on f.47r of Lbs 2477 4to (1868–1873), found opposite his first appearance in the text on f.46v and depicting him in the garments described as he departs home.

Many thanks to Sigríður Hjördís Jörundsdóttir and the team at Handritadeild Landsbókasafns Íslands (Manuscripts Department at the National Library of Iceland) for kindly providing access to the manuscript, scanning it and granting permission for the image to be reproduced.

CONTENTS

INTRODUCTION	v
1. Genre	vi
2. Sources and Influences	xi
2a. *Þiðreks saga af Bern*	xi
2b. *Parcevals saga*	xiii
2c. *Bósa saga ok Herrauðs*	xv
2d. *Hálfdanar saga Eysteinssonar*	xxi
2e. *Eskja* and the Transmission of Cinderella in Old Norse Literature	xxviii
2e.i. *Eskja*	xxxi
2e.ii. *Ragnars saga*	xxxv
2e.iii. *Hálfdanar saga Eysteinssonar*	xxxvii
2e.iv. The Cinder-name	xliii
3, Manuscripts and Editions	xlix
Bibliography	lx
TEXT AND TRANSLATION	1

INTRODUCTION

Vilmundar saga viðutan 'The Saga of Vilmundur the Outsider' is a late-medieval Icelandic saga which was probably written in the fourteenth century, although it only survives in manuscripts from the fifteenth century onwards. The saga, an entertaining romance set in Garðaríki (the Kievan Rus'), details the adventures of Vilmundur *viðutan* (literally 'Vilmundur from the outside'),[1] the rustic son of a farmer whose rise through society is characterised by a combination of unrefined social etiquette and raw athletic prowess.

Vilmundar saga enjoyed enduring popularity in Iceland, surviving in some form in fifty-four known manuscripts, which were produced between the fifteenth and nineteenth centuries. Three of these are medieval manuscripts from the fifteenth century. The Vilmundur tradition also spawned five individual sets of *rímur*, the genre of Icelandic rhymed poems that became extremely popular between the fifteenth and nineteenth centuries. Vilmundur is also referenced in texts outside his own tradition: he is listed alongside numerous saga heroes—most of whom are from romance sagas—in the sixteenth-century poem *Allra kappa kvæði*, and he is named at the end of *Bósa saga ok Herrauðs*, another legendary romance probably written in the fourteenth century, as the grandson of its hero, Bósi. This genealogical connection has uniquely significant implications for *Vilmundar saga*, and will be discussed later.

In terms of scholarly reception, however, the saga—ironically, like Vilmundur himself—has remained on the periphery. Perhaps because of the saga's primary setting, Garðaríki, it seems to have had little place in the nationalistic agendas of the Swedish and Danish scholars of the seventeenth century; and it was likewise ignored by most Icelandic scholars of the early twentieth century, who were generally dismissive of the formulaically fantastic sagas belonging to what they perceived to be the period of decline following the 'Golden Age' of saga writing in the thirteenth century. In recent decades, there has been a welcome revival of scholarly interest in the fantastic saga genres, the *fornaldarsögur* and *riddarasögur*, but because *Vilmundar saga* occupies a complex position between the two

---

[1] To conform with the normalisation of the text of *Vilmundar saga* in this edition (see Section 3), names of characters in the saga, as well as quotations from it, appear in this introduction as they do in the text. Thus the names *Vilmundur* and *Kolur* appear with the epenthetic vowel rather than as *Vilmundr* and *Kolr* as in standardised Old Norse. The titles of sagas referred to in this introduction and in the notes to the text are normalised according to the conventions used in Guðni Jónsson's 1954 *fornaldarsögur* edition.

groups it has not benefitted from this revival as much as it deserves to. The question of genre will be discussed in Section 1 of this introduction. An accessible text and English translation of *Vilmundar saga* should be of interest not only to the scholar of Old Norse, or indeed of medieval romance, but also to folklorists and the general reader, because the saga holds a unique and extraordinary position in European folklore. Not only is it arguably 'the first appearance of Cinderella in Iceland' (Einar Ólafur Sveinsson 2003, 235)—a claim which will be qualified in Sections 2.e.iii and 2.e.iv—but it is also, by between two and three centuries, the earliest known Cinderella variant in the world which contains a cinder-name, that is, a name relating to work at the hearth. Because of this, *Vilmundar saga* might even be considered the earliest incarnation of the modern Cinderella. In fact, the saga's cinder-name, Öskubuska, is still the name for Cinderella in modern Icelandic. Until very recently the saga has escaped the attention of Cinderella scholarship, and it is not discussed in the two most important scholarly works on the Cinderella tale type: no accessible edition was available to Marian Roalfe Cox as she compiled her remarkable collection of Cinderella variants, published in 1893; while in 1951 Anna Birgitta Rooth, in her seminal doctoral thesis on the worldwide development of 'the Cinderella cycle', seems to have had access only to the plot summary of *Vilmundar saga* in Franz Schröder's edition of *Hálfdanar saga Eysteinssonar* (Rooth 1980, 110, n. 41).[2] As far as research on variants of the Cinderella tale type goes, then, *Vilmundar saga* is very much the latecomer to the party, and it is hoped that this volume will help to redress this.

1. Genre

The question of genre is an important one with regard to *Vilmundar saga*, because it has had a large impact on the saga's scholarly reception. The saga may be described, quite simply, as a legendary romance, and it was part of the 'trend towards the fantastic and the fictive' in the fourteenth century (Meulengracht Sørensen 2000, 25), a trend that produced most of the sagas that modern scholars refer to as *fornaldarsögur* ('stories of an ancient time', or mythical-heroic sagas) and *riddarasögur* ('stories of

---

[2] At the time of Rooth's doctoral thesis only one edition of *Vilmundar saga* had been published: Guðmundur Hjartarson's popular edition of 1878. This edition was (and remains) notoriously difficult to get hold of—even Schröder, in his edition of *Hálfdanar saga Eysteinssonar*, spoke of the *sehr schwer zugänglichen isländischen druck von Guðmundur Hjartarson* 'very difficult-to-obtain printed Icelandic edition by Guðmundur Hjartarson' (Schröder 1917, 82, n. 1). The full editorial history of *Vilmundar saga* will be discussed in Section 3 of this introduction.

knights', or romance sagas). These taxonomic categorisations, however, are not medieval (even if the term *riddarasaga* has a medieval attestation in *Mágus saga jarls*), and *fornaldarsögur* travelled freely with *riddarasögur* in medieval and post-medieval manuscripts alike (Driscoll 2005, 193–94).

A brief description of the two corpora will be useful here. The *riddarasögur* are commonly divided into two subsections. The first group, the 'translated *riddarasögur*', comprises texts translated from continental sources. Sources for the translated *riddarasögur* are exceptionally diverse, including works of legendary history, such as Geoffrey of Monmouth's *Historia Regum Britanniae* and Walter de Châtillon's *Alexandreis*; romances, including the Arthurian romances of Chrétien de Troyes, which were translated into Old Norse at the behest of King Hákon Hákonarson (who ruled Norway from 1217 to 1263); the *lais* of Marie de France; and even the comedic play *Pamphilus de amore*. The second group, the 'indigenous *riddarasögur*', comprises original works composed in Iceland from the fourteenth century onwards. This group, which includes *Vilmundar saga*, is less diverse in style, but nonetheless includes sagas which show varying degrees of direct continental influence. For instance, the prologue of *Klári saga* claims that the saga was translated from a Latin original (Cederschiöld 1907, 1), and scholars' uncertainty over this claim has led to the saga being variously categorised as a translated *riddarasaga* and an indigenous one (Hughes 2008, 135–36).[3]

The term *fornaldarsaga* was coined in 1829 by the Danish scholar Carl Christian Rafn, who published thirty-one sagas in his three-volume *Fornaldar sögur Nordrlanda*.[4] Although he coined the term, he was not the first to group these thirty-one sagas together in print. His corpus was heavily influenced by that of Peter Erasmus Müller in the second volume of his three-volume *Sagabibliothek*, a fact to which Philip Lavender recently drew attention (Lavender 2015b, 526–51). It was Müller who was responsible for designating what would later become known as the *fornaldarsaga* corpus, and Müller's 'open-handed approach to saga selection' is therefore responsible for one of the most prominent and

---

[3] For a survey of the problems of the translated-indigenous divide in categorising *riddarasögur*, see Driscoll 2005, 191–94.

[4] Rafn's corpus was to be expanded to thirty-four texts in Bjarni Vilhjálmsson and Guðni Jónsson's three-volume edition *Fornaldarsögur Norðurlanda*, published in 1943–44. The texts added were *Yngvars saga víðförla*, *Tóka þáttr Tókasonar*, *Helga þáttr Þórissonar* and *Þorsteins þáttr bæjarmagns*, while *Eiríks saga víðförla* was demoted to an appendix. When Guðni Jónsson reprinted this edition as the four-volume *Fornaldar Sögur Norðurlanda* in 1954–59, *Eiríks saga* was removed altogether.

enduring aspects of the corpus: the diversity of the texts within it (Lavender 2015b, 532).[5] At one end of the scale, we find 'traditional' *fornaldarsögur*, which were based on pre-existing poetry deriving from ancient Germanic legends. These sagas, which include *Völsunga saga* and *Hálfs saga ok Hálfsrekka*, are all prosimetric, multigenerational and almost always tragic in nature. By contrast, a number of young *fornaldarsögur*—written from the fourteenth century onwards and with no substantial basis in ancient heroic legends—follow the linear trajectory and dialectical perspective of romance, in that they revolve around the quests of one or two heroes. These sagas, which include *Göngu-Hrólfs saga*, have a 'fondness for the fabulous, stock characters, lengthy battle scenes' (Driscoll 2003, 257), and they always have a comic ending—that is to say, the hero marries a princess and all ends well.[6]

Rafn's corpus was made up of those sagas *er greina frá atburðum þeim, er orðit hafa hér á Norðrlöndum, áðr enn Island bygðist á 9du öld* 'which tell of those events which have taken place here in the Northern lands, before Iceland was settled in the ninth century' (Rafn 1829, I v). As Lavender (2015b, 535) demonstrated, this oft-quoted statement of Rafn's was probably based on Müller's own description of the second volume of his *Sagabibliothek* as consisting of *alle mythiske Sagaer, de nemlig, der indeholde Sagn om hvad der er skeet i Norden for Islands bebyggelse* 'all mythical sagas, namely those which include narrative material about what has happened in the North before the settlement of Iceland' (Müller 1817–20, I xvi). By *i Norden* and *hér á Norðrlöndum*, Müller and Rafn were both referring to Scandinavia, but even this basic parameter is not without its problems; one of the most exaggeratedly fantastical and romance-like *fornaldarsögur*, *Hjálmþés saga ok Ölvis*, is based not in a real Scandinavian location, but in a generic kingdom called Mannheimar (literally 'Homes of Man').[7] This arbitrary geographical criterion is problematic in that it separates the romance-like *fornaldarsögur* from some indigenous *riddarasögur* which are otherwise very similar to them in all stylistic and structural aspects. Scholars have applied various terms to this group of indigenous

---

[5] For a broad review of scholarship on the question of genre in the *fornaldarsögur*, see Mitchell 1991, 8–32. For a recent round-table discussion on the subject, see Quinn et al. 2006, 276–96.

[6] For a succinct comparison between these two types of *fornaldarsögur* using Alistair Fowler's theory of genre, see Rowe's contribution in Quinn et al. 2006, 284–86.

[7] Although Mannheimar is given as a name for Sweden in *Ynglinga saga*, there is no evidence that it is meant to be equated with Sweden in *Hjálmþés saga*.

riddarasögur, such as *lygisögur* and *Märchensagas* (Schier 1970, 105–15; Glauser 1983, 10–22), but for various reasons these are not in universal usage (Driscoll 2005, 190–91). Of the indigenous *riddarasögur*, six in particular are seen as 'borderline *fornaldarsögur*', in that their action, despite occurring outside Scandinavia, is set 'in a Viking, rather than a chivalric, milieu' (Driscoll 2005, 191). These are *Ála flekks saga*, *Hrings saga ok Tryggva*, *Sigrgarðs saga frækna*, *Sigurðar saga fóts*, *Vilmundar saga viðutan* and *Þjalar-Jóns saga*.[8] Of these, *Ála flekks saga*, *Sigurðar saga fóts* and *Vilmundar saga* share a rare distinction among *riddarasögur*: they are distantly connected to Scandinavia through explicit genealogical relations to *fornaldarsaga* heroes. Áli of *Ála flekks saga* is the grandson of Hálfdan of *Hálfdanar saga Brönufóstra*; Ásmundr Húnakappi of *Sigurðar saga fóts* is grandfather of Ásmundr and Hildibrandr Húnakappi of *Ásmundar saga kappabana*; while Vilmundur of *Vilmundar saga* is the grandson of Bósi of *Bósa saga*, a connection which will be discussed in Section 2c of this introduction. *Vilmundar saga*'s connections to *fornaldarsögur* run deeper than this. As will be seen in Section 2, it has a particularly strong connection to the corpus of legendary sagas because its two strongest literary influences are both from *fornaldarsögur*: *Bósa saga* and *Hálfdanar saga Eysteinssonar*. The saga also contains individual elements that are common in *fornaldarsögur* but far rarer in *riddarasögur*: Vilmundur's status as a commoner; his prophetic dream featuring a bear and a boar, two symbolic animals from the select bestiary of *fornaldarsaga* dreams (Lönnroth 2002, 56–57); and the use of Garðaríki as a setting of some importance (see Section 2d).[9] Yet while many *fornaldarsögur* feature Garðaríki, none is set entirely in it. Therefore, in spite of its obvious thematic and stylistic similarities to *fornaldarsögur*, *Vilmundar saga* did not fit the geographical criterion required for inclusion in Müller's or Rafn's corpora, and it has never been inducted into the 'canon' since. Partly because of this, the saga

---

[8] Three of these sagas have recently been translated into English for the first time: *Sigurðar saga fóts* by Alaric Hall et al. (2010), *Sigrgarðs saga frækna* by Hall et al. (2013) and *Þjalar-Jóns saga* by Philip Lavender (2016). For a recent English translation of *Ála flekks saga*, see Hui et al. (2018). No English translation has been made of the medieval *Hrings saga ok Tryggva*, which only survives in fragments, or of its post-medieval reconstruction.

[9] On a tangential note, it is intriguing that the saga contains another striking echo of Scandinavia—not in its geographical setting but in a geological landform. This echo is much closer to home for the saga author, for amidst the castles and turrets that are typical of romance, we find a *laug*, a hot spring, near which Vilmundur finds Sóley's shoe. These springs remain a distinctive part of Iceland's landscape today.

has virtually never been discussed alongside *fornaldarsögur*, even during the revival of interest in the corpus in recent decades.

During the seventeenth and eighteenth centuries, editions of many *fornaldarsögur* were produced by Swedish scholars as 'part of the propaganda war between Sweden and Denmark as to which country had the more glorious past' (Driscoll 2003, 260), and at least one editor saw a connection between *Vilmundar saga* and these sagas. In Guðmundur Ólafsson's introduction to his 1694 Swedish edition of *Sturlaugs saga starfsama*, we find *Vilmundar saga* named alongside other supposedly truthful and historical *fornaldarsögur*, namely *Hervarar saga*, *Völsunga saga*, *Hálfdanar saga Eysteinssonar*, *Þorsteins saga Víkingssonar*, *Friðþjófs saga*, *Göngu-Hrólfs saga* and *Hrómundar saga Gripssonar* (Lavender 2014, 204–05). *Vilmundar saga* is the only saga in this list set outside Scandinavia, and Philip Lavender suggests that it is included because Vilmundur's father Sviði is a recurring character featuring in several other *fornaldarsögur*, namely *Bósa saga*, *Hálfdanar saga Eysteinssonar* and *Illuga saga Gríðarfóstra* (Lavender 2014, 227–28). In *Bósa saga*, Sviði is named as the son of the Gautish hero Bósi. This, according to Lavender, would make Vilmundur the son of an 'ancient Swede', and accordingly 'a type of Swedish hero by blood' (2014, 228). Guðmundur's interest in *Vilmundar saga*, therefore, was probably mostly based on the saga hero's indirect connection to Sweden.

In spite of Guðmundur's interest, however, no edition of *Vilmundar saga* was produced as part of this wave of nationalism. Whether or not Guðmundur intended to publish it, he died in 1695, a year after his edition of *Sturlaugs saga* was published. More generally, the lack of contemporary scholarly interest in *Vilmundar saga* was probably due to the fact that the saga does not directly involve a Scandinavian country. Certainly this was the sticking point for the Danish historian Peter Frederik Suhm (1728–98). On the fly-leaf of the manuscript NKS 1250 fol.,[10] copied from the medieval AM 586 4to between 1771 and 1779,[11] Suhm wrote the following about *Vilmundar saga* (Loth 1977, 14):

> Er en fabel, hvori intet forekommer om vort Norden. Skrevet uden tvil i det 14 eller 15 sæculo.

[10] The 'NKS' shelfmark refers to a manuscript from the New Royal Collection (*Ny kongelig Samling*) in Denmark, held in the National Library of Denmark.

[11] The 'AM' shelfmark indicates that the manuscript was part of the great collection of Árni Magnússon (1663–1730), which has since been divided between the Arnamagnæan Institute in Copenhagen and the Árni Magnússon Institute in Reykjavik. AM 586 4to is now housed in Reykjavik.

It is a fable, with nothing in it concerning our northern world. Doubtless written in the fourteenth or fifteenth century.

It is interesting that *Vilmundar saga*'s non-Scandinavian setting should be the main criterion by which Suhm dismissed it, because if we consider this alongside the reason for Guðmundur's interest, it fully encapsulates the paradox at the root of the saga: its setting is northern but not Scandinavian, its hero descended from Sweden but born and bred in Russia. Thus, even before Müller designated what would become the *fornaldarsaga* corpus along geographical lines in the nineteenth century, *Vilmundar saga* was already problematising this divide. It would not be wide of the mark for us as modern scholars to regard *Vilmundar saga* as a *fornaldarsaga* set a mere five hundred miles too far east, or as a Russia-based spin-off of the Scandinavia-based romances. Indeed, our understanding of both the saga and the canon might be furthered were we to do so.

2. Sources and Influences

Scholars of the early twentieth century were extremely dismissive of the Norse romances, deeming them derivative, uncreative and unaesthetic (Kalinke 1985, 316–17). That these sagas were considered unsatisfactory in every regard is evident from W. P. Ker's infamous remark that 'they are among the dreariest things ever made by human fancy' (1908, 282). However heavy-handed this blanket denigration may seem today, the charge that the romances are derivative is irrefutable, and *Vilmundar saga* is no exception. It borrowed heavily and obviously from a number of literary sources, so that their clear influence can be identified on many levels, from the stylistic, to the structural, to the thematic. In his dissertation on *Vilmundar saga*, Einar Sigurðsson identified four key influences (1962, 23–68): *Þiðreks saga af Bern*, *Parcevals saga*, *Bósa saga* and *Hálfdanar saga Eysteinssonar*.[12] All four of these sagas will be discussed, as well as another source which has not previously been identified, but which is of immense significance: *Eskja*, which forms part of the *Strengleikar* compilation.

2a. Þiðreks saga af Bern

Þiðreks saga is a lengthy compilation of legends relating to Dietrich von Bern which was translated in Norway in the thirteenth century, probably

---

[12] Einar also highlighted a relatively minor connection between *Vilmundar saga* and two of the younger (that is, fourteenth-century) *Íslendingasögur*, *Kjalnesinga saga* and *Finnboga saga ramma* (1962, 60–62).

from a Low German source (Kalinke 2011, 158). It is known to have influenced a number of Icelandic sagas of different genres, including *Íslendingasögur* (Mundt 1973), *riddarasögur* such as *Erex saga* (Bornholdt 2011, 115) and *fornaldarsögur* such as *Ragnars saga loðbrókar* (McTurk 1977) and *Völsunga saga* (Finch 1965, ix–xxxii), which borrowed from it the entire chapter on Sigurðr's appearance following his slaying of the dragon Fáfnir. *Vilmundar saga* seems to have borrowed specifically from *Þiðreks saga*'s story of Þéttleifr the Dane (Einar Sigurðsson 1962, 54), although a possible connection to the story of Ósantrix and Oda, another story in the compilation, will be discussed in Section 2e.iii. The most obvious of *Vilmundar saga*'s borrowings come in the form of action scenes. For instance, Þéttleifr's stone-throwing competition with Valtari is described as follows in *Þiðreks saga* (Bertelsen 1905–11, 246–47):

> Ganga þeir nv vt a voll noccorn oc taca stein einn er eigi stoð minna en. ij. scip pvnd. þann stein toc valtari oc kastaði fra ser. ix. fet. En þetleifr kastar .x. fet. Nv kastar valtari .xiij. fet. þa kastar þetleifr xviij. fet. Nv vill valtari eigi optaʀ til ganga
>
> Now they go out to a certain field and take a stone weighing no less than two *skippund*. Valtari took the stone and cast it nine feet from himself, but Þéttleifr cast it ten feet. Then Valtari casts it thirteen feet, but Þéttleifr casts it eighteen feet. Now Valtari does not wish to continue any longer.

Apart from minor differences in the measurements, Vilmundur's stone-throwing competition with Hjarrandi in chapter 12 of *Vilmundar saga* is identically choreographed: the challenger (in both cases having just eaten very heartily) out-throws the distinguished representative of the royal court on two occasions, thus forcing him to yield.[13] Immediately after their stone-throwing competition, Þéttleifr and Valtari compete in spear-throwing (Bertelsen 1905–11, 247):

---

[13] Vilmundur bears a resemblance not just to Þéttleifr, but also to another Danish hero: the eponymous protagonist of the Middle English verse romance *Havelok the Dane*. Havelok, like Vilmundur, is notable for his exceptional physical prowess, as we are told in lines 989–90: *Jn Engelond was non hise per / Of strengþe þat euere kam him ner* 'In England he had no equal / in strength who ever came close to him' (Smithers 1987, 32). In this very scene, Havelok also triumphs in wrestling and stone-throwing competitions, two activities that Vilmundur competes in as well, against Ruddi and Hjarrandi respectively. There are also some thematic similarities; if Havelok is to be seen as 'the embodiment of the ideal king from the point of view of the lower classes' (Staines 1976, 623), then the vindication of Vilmundur's refusal to conform to social norms, as discussed in Section 2c, might be read in a similar light.

Nv skytr valtari þesso scapti ivir konongs holl sva at annaʀr endir kœmr niðr a hallarveginvm. Nv mæltv allir þeir menn er þetta sa at fvrðv sterklega er scotið. þetleifr tecr nv scaptit oc skytr aftr ivir hollena oc er hann hevir scotit þa rennr hann igegnvm hollina er tvidyr var oc toc a lopti spiotscaptit oc gengr nv ibrot við sva bvit.

Now Valtari throws this shaft over the king's hall so that one end comes down in the wall of the hall. Then everyone who saw that said that the throw was wonderfully strong. Now Þéttleifr takes the shaft and throws it back into the hall, and when he has shot it, he runs through the double-doored hall, caught the spear-shaft in the air, and then walks outside in this manner.

Barring minor differences in detail, this turn of events matches Vilmundur and Hjarrandi's own spear-throwing competition at the beginning of chapter 13, which also takes place immediately after the stone-throwing. Apart from this extended scene, there are other instances of parallel choreography between the two sagas, such as Þéttleifr's grapple with Sigurðr grikr's strong daughter (Bertelsen 1905–11, 228–29), which mirrors Vilmundur's brief struggle with Sóley-in-disguise in chapter 11 of *Vilmundar saga*, each of them ending in the hero squeezing his opponent's neck and hand so hard that tears flow from her eyes and blood from her nails. The extent of the influence of *Þiðreks saga* on *Vilmundar saga* is thus primarily textual, as demonstrated by the close syntactic correspondences between them.

2b. *Parcevals saga*

Another significant source for *Vilmundar saga* was *Parcevals saga*, the Old Norse translation of Chrétien de Troyes's unfinished verse romance *Perceval*, which was composed in the twelfth century. It is thought to have been translated along with Thomas of Britain's *Tristan* and Chrétien's *Yvain* (into the Old Norse *Tristrams saga ok Ísöndar* and *Ívens saga* respectively) at the behest of King Hákon Hákonarson (Kalinke 1999, 105). The similarity that Vilmundur as a character bears to Perceval has been previously noted by scholars (for example Schlauch 1934, 167, Einar Sigurðsson 1962, 43–53 and McKinnell 2005, 188), and this is clearest in the portrayal of Vilmundur's youth and upbringing. In Chrétien's *Perceval* and subsequent adaptations of the legend, Perceval is characterised by his initial naivety, having grown up in a forest in isolation, with only his mother for company. Vilmundur is very similar in this regard, growing up in a forest until the age of twenty without any human contact other than with his parents. This reclusive upbringing is almost inevitably foregrounded when the protagonists first interact with other humans. In *Perceval*, the young hero is so awestruck at encountering a fully armoured knight for the first time that he asks him if he is God. This episode is also recounted in chapter 1 of *Parcevals saga* (Kalinke 1999, 108–09):

> En honum varð ekki annat á munni en spyrja riddarann, ef hann væri guð; kvað móður sína hafa sagt sér at ekki væri jafn fagrt sem guð.
>
> But he could find nothing to say other than to ask the knight if he were God; he said his mother had told him that nothing was so beautiful as God.

Similarly, in *Vilmundar saga*, the young Vilmundur's worldview is overwhelmingly directed by the narrow scope of parental guidance. Having been told by his parents in chapter 8 that all the men from stories are dead, but that trolls and elves still exist, he asks the first non-parental human with whom he ever converses—Princess Gullbrá in chapter 9—whether she is *maður eður tröll, eður álfkona* 'a human or a troll or an elf-lady'. Gullbrá takes this with good-natured amusement, which only emphasises Vilmundur's naive ignorance. Although Margaret Schlauch downplayed the strength of the influence of the Perceval tradition on *Vilmundar saga*, writing that 'the Vilmundar saga seems to owe more to folk-tales about a simpleton from the country, than to the romance [Chrétien de Troyes's *Perceval*]' (1934, 167), the specific parallels in the example above suggest direct influence. So too do the parallel portrayals of the fathers of Parceval and Vilmundur. It is worth noting that Parceval's father's career takes a different turn in *Parcevals saga* from that in Chrétien's *Perceval*, in that he becomes a farmer after his adventures as a knight. This is a minor biographical addition, but it is one that is paralleled and expanded on in Vilmundur's father Sviði, whose goat Gæfa is the catalyst for Vilmundur's departure into the wider world. Another noteworthy peculiarity in the description of Parceval's father in *Parcevals saga*—one of the few things said about him at all—is that he is said to have taught Parceval shooting and swordsmanship. At the beginning of the saga, we are told about Parceval's father that

> Hann hafði áðr kent honum skot ok skylmingar, ok svá kunni hann gaflökum at skjóta svá at þrjú váru á lopti senn.
>
> His father had already taught him [Parceval] archery and swordplay, and he could throw javelins so that three were in the air at once. (Kalinke 1999, 108–09)

This detail—which does not appear in Chrétien's *Perceval*—has some significance. As in Chrétien's romance, Parceval's knightly career begins with his slaying of the Red Knight, which is accomplished with a javelin

(Kalinke 1999, 116–19). The implication is that he is able to accomplish this feat because of his proficiency in a chivalric skill taught to him by his father, a former knight. Thus, despite the young Parceval's pronounced lack of knightly training—for instance, he displays his self-frustrating ignorance of the basic mechanics of armour immediately after killing the Red Knight—he is shown to have chivalric potential owing to his limited but not meagre skills training. Indeed, Parceval continues to be invariably successful at combat throughout the saga.

This idea of fatherly chivalric training is paralleled in *Vilmundar saga*. Like Parceval's father, Vilmundur's father Sviði is also a warrior-turned-farmer who teaches Vilmundur skills that prove to be important throughout the rest of the saga (*Vilmundar saga*, chapter 8):

> Faðir hans hafði verið hinn mesti kappi, og því kenndi hann syni sínum íþróttir, sund og tafl og að skjóta og að skylmazt með skjölld og sverð.

> His [Vilmundur's] father had been a great champion, and so he taught his son his skills: swimming and chess, shooting and fencing with shield and sword.

In chapters 12 and 13 Vilmundur competes against Hjarrandi in stone-casting, spear-throwing and swimming, and his success not only saves him from any punishment for trespassing, but also wins him Hjarrandi's approval and foster-brothership. This is the first point at which Vilmundur is accepted into society; his proficiency in skills offsets his social naivety and facilitates his rise through society. Like Parceval's, therefore, part of Vilmundur's potential as a diamond-in-the-rough comes from his father's training, and this training proves to be the means by which he integrates himself into society. Thus, Parceval's and Vilmundur's fathers share the same character history and narrative function: they are both farmers with a respectable former career which enables them to pass their sons certain important chivalric skills, and whose relocation to a secluded forest leaves their sons room to climb the social ladder.

2c. *Bósa saga ok Herrauðs*

While *Vilmundar saga*'s parallels with *Parcevals saga* and *Þiðreks saga* are mainly limited to individual episodes, it shares deeper connections with *Bósa saga*. Bósi, the primary protagonist of that saga, has a direct genealogical relationship with Vilmundur, the significance of which cannot be overstated. At the end of *Bósa saga*, we are told of Bósi after he becomes king of Bjarmaland (Jiriczek 1893, 62):

> Hann átti son við frillu sinni, þeirri er hann herti jarlinn hjá; sá hét Sviði hinn sókndjarfi, hann var faðir Vilmundar viðutan.

He had a son with his mistress, the one with whom he had 'hardened his jarl';[14] he was called Sviði hinn sókndjarfi 'the Battle-Bold', and he was the father of Vilmundr viðutan.[15]

This connection is given towards the end of two out of the three fifteenth-century witnesses of *Bósa saga*, AM 586 4to and AM 577 4to (the third, AM 343 a 4to, does not preserve the ending of *Bósa saga*).[16] As will be discussed in Section 3, these three manuscripts are the earliest witnesses of both *Bósa saga* and *Vilmundar saga*. In AM 586 4to (henceforth 586), which forms the base text of this edition, *Vilmundar saga* immediately follows *Bósa saga*, and it reiterates the same genealogical connection (*Vilmundar saga*, chapter 9):

> Kall bjó í afdal langt í burt frá öðrum mönnum. Hann hét Sviði hinn sókndjarfi, son Bögu-Bósa. Kelling hans hét Herborg. Þau áttu son þann er Vilmundur er nefndur.
>
> There was a farmer who lived in a remote valley far away from other men. He was called Sviði hinn sókndjarfi, son of Bögu-Bósi. His wife was called Herborg. They had a son named Vilmundur.

It should be noted that while this Bósi-Vilmundur connection is not explicitly mentioned in the text of *Vilmundar saga* found in AM 577 4to (henceforth 577), where Sviði is introduced without the cognomen *hinn sókndjarfi* or his parentage, this is unlikely to be a significant omission, since the text of *Bósa saga* in the same manuscript mentions that Sviði was Bósi's son, and Vilmundur Bósi's grandson.[17] Thus, supported by the fact that the earliest three

---

[14] In *Bósa saga*, Bósi has three one-night stands, each of which is described (with sordid relish) through a different sexual metaphor. This particular encounter with the unnamed daughter of a farmer named Hóketill, in which Sviði is conceived, is the first of Bósi's three sexual escapades.

[15] Intriguingly, as Lavender notes, Sviði hinn sókndjarfi is attested in other *fornaldarsögur*: in *Hálfdanar saga Eysteinssonar*, in which he is a companion of the eponymous Hálfdan, as well as in some manuscript witnesses of *Illuga saga Gríðarfóstra*, which state that Sviði hinn sókndjarfi is also the father of the eponymous Illugi, which would suggest a blood relationship between Illugi and Vilmundur (Lavender 2015a, 3). However, unlike Vilmundur, Illugi is not mentioned in connection with Sviði at the end of *Bósa saga*.

[16] These three manuscripts are now housed in Reykjavik.

[17] In his edition of *Bósa saga*, Otto Luitpold Jiriczek argued that the mention of Vilmundur's relation to Bósi in the text of *Vilmundar saga* in 586, and lack thereof in 577, showed that the relationship was only created later in the development of the two sagas' traditions: *so ist eben der Umstand, dass es ein Zusatz einer Hdschr. ist, Beweis, dass eine wirkliche Verbindung der zwei Sagas ursprünglich nicht bestanden hat, vielmehr erst später von der Vilm.-s. [Vilmundar saga] ausgieng, und aus dieser in die B.-S. [Bósa saga] eindrang* 'thus the fact that it is an addition

extant manuscript witnesses of *Vilmundar saga* also happen to be the earliest three extant witnesses of *Bósa saga*, it is clear that by the second half of the fifteenth century at the latest, the Vilmundur tradition had already been well established, and that the Vilmundur and Bósi traditions were already connected.

The two sagas also share clear literary similarities. One example of this is in their character configuration. Like Vilmundur and Parceval, Bósi is born not to a king, but to a former warrior, and is thus of common stock. After killing the king's bastard son following provocation, he is sentenced to death by the king, but an intervention from his foster-mother Busla reduces his punishment and instead has him cast out of the kingdom and sent abroad on a perilous quest. Throughout the saga, Bósi has the support of Herrauðr, his foster-brother and the king's (legitimate) son. The result of their successful adventures is that Bósi achieves reconciliation with the king before the latter's death, and eventually marries a princess to become a king in his own right (albeit over Bjarmaland, 'Permia' rather than his native Gautland). Similarly, Vilmundur is of common stock and upbringing,[18] and his father is also a former warrior. His eventual blood-brother, Hjarrandi, is also a prince, who helps to facilitate Vilmundur's reconciliation with King Vísivalldur at the end of the saga, a reconciliation which results in Vilmundur marrying Princess Sóley and becoming a duke. The similarities in character configuration are clear, but one of these similarities deserves further comment.

Although sagas of two exclusive blood-brothers are not uncommon in *fornaldarsögur* and *riddarasögur*,[19] *Bósa saga* and *Vilmundar saga*

---

to one manuscript is proof that a true connection between the two sagas did not originally exist, but only came later from *Vilm[undar] saga* and entered *B[ósa] s[aga]* from there' (Jiriczek 1893, 53). However, this seems to be too large an assumption to make given that the 577 text of *Bósa saga* does mention Vilmundur in the final chapter. It should also be noted that this omission was not an issue for several post-medieval manuscripts of *Vilmundar saga*, which derive from one or more manuscript(s) closely related to the 577 text (as discussed in Section 3), and therefore lack any mention of Bósi in the introduction of Vilmundur, but nonetheless refer to Vilmundur as Bósi's grandson in the rubric or epilogue.

[18] Since Bósi spends only one evening with Hóketill's unnamed daughter, we can assume that Sviði is conceived in that night, and therefore prior to Bósi becoming king of Bjarmaland. Such technicalities aside, there is no indication in *Vilmundar saga* that Vilmundur is considered to be of royal heritage because of his descent from Bósi.

[19] In the corpus of *fornaldarsögur*, we find *Egils saga einhenda ok Ásmundar berserkjabana* and *Hjálmþés saga ok Ölvis*; in the borderline *fornaldarsögur*, *Þjalar-Jóns saga*; in the indigenous *riddarasögur*, *Jarlmanns saga ok Hermanns*, *Konráðs saga keisarasonar*, *Saulus saga ok Nikanors* and *Viktors saga ok Blávus*; and in the translated *riddarasögur*, *Amicus saga ok Amilíus*.

are the only two sagas in these corpora in which the exclusive blood-brotherhood is between a prince and a commoner. One of the significant effects of this is that an extra layer of complexity is added to the two commoner-heroes, Bósi and Vilmundur: thanks to his blue-blooded blood-brother, each can be 'in' society without being 'of' it. Both Bósi and Vilmundur possess characteristically antisocial traits that persist even through to their eventual integration into roles of social authority. At the end of his saga, Bósi becomes king over Bjarmaland, a stereotypical place of otherness in Old Norse literature, rather than his Scandinavian homeland, Gautland. He achieves this with characteristic cunning, using exactly the same method by which he has achieved both of his other major successes: by sleeping with a farmer's daughter to gain information about a certain valuable target, before stealing that target and escaping. On the third such occasion, his target is Princess Edda of Bjarmaland, legally the heir to the throne, which becomes vacant with her father's death. Bósi's (forced) marriage to Edda proves to be the principal basis of his successful claim to the throne of Bjarmaland in the final chapter of the saga. Thus, Bósi's ascent to the throne of Bjarmaland is a direct result of his idiosyncratic unorthodoxy, and his rise to nobility takes place on his own terms, with the essence of his character remaining uncompromised.

Vilmundur is characterised by uncompromising bluntness throughout the saga, and this is most clearly highlighted in his interactions with King Vísivalldur. In chapter 10, Vilmundur explains to Princess Gullbrá that he is unfamiliar with the concept of 'king', providing the platform for his consequent lack of deference towards Vísivalldur throughout the rest of the saga—a characteristic emphasised through contradistinction with the ever-courteous Prince Guðifreyr of Galicia (who, in his impressive verbosity, employs the royal plural almost invariably). Vilmundur's actions are equally blunt, and this is most significant when he angers Vísivalldur by throwing the bloodied head of 'Sóley' onto his table in chapter 18. Vísivalldur himself makes it clear that Vilmundur's tactless handling of the matter is to blame for his exile (*Vilmundar saga*, chapter 18):

'því að þó að ég villda mína dóttur dauða fyrir sín illbrigði, þá má ég ei þá skamm þola, að hennar blóð renni yfir mín borð, svo sem það kalli á mig til hefndar eptir sig. Því skal Vilmundur eigi fyrir mín augu koma að svo búnu mínu lyndi.'

'for although I wanted my daughter dead because of her misdeeds, I cannot endure the shame of her blood running over my tables, as if it urges me to avenge it. Because of this disgrace, Vilmundur must never again come into my sight.'

This conflict between Vísivalldur and Vilmundur is the last to be resolved in the saga, yet the resolution comes about with the acquiescence of the king rather than the hero. At no point does Vilmundur apologise to the king, whose fury is quite understandable; instead, the rift is mended by Prince Hjarrandi's persuasion of the king to forgive Vilmundur and placate him by offering him the title of duke, a third of Garðaríki and (the real) Sóley in marriage. Thus, even the greatest offence born of Vilmundur's indecorum is somewhat vindicated. Like Bósi, the consistency of his unorthodox characteristics punctuates his eventual rise to social acceptance and a position of power.

Bósi and Vilmundur thus share a very specific career trajectory: each of them is a protagonist of common blood; each finds himself in a position of social ostracism at a young age; each retains the persistent support of a single blood-brother who is a prince, who defends him against the king and represents his anchor to society and his route to social redemption; each proves his worth to society through the accomplishment of heroic deeds; and each is ultimately rewarded with social reconciliation, marriage and a position of nobility, while maintaining his integral idiosyncrasies.

It has already been mentioned that the three oldest extant manuscripts containing *Vilmundar saga* also happen to be the three oldest containing *Bósa saga*: 343a, 577 and 586. These manuscripts will be discussed further in Section 3, but it is interesting to note that the scribe of the two sagas in 586 considered them to be especially good bookfellows. Not only do they appear consecutively in the manuscript, but each of them ends with an extended and provocative *explicit* not found in its other medieval manuscripts. The 586 text of *Vilmundar saga* ends as follows:

> Og endum vér svo sögu Vilmundar viðutan með því álykarorði af þeim, sem skrifað hefir, að sá, sem lesið hefir, og hinir, sem til hafa hlýtt, og allir þeir, sem eigi eru svo ríkir, að þeir eigi kongi vorum skatt að gjallda, þá kyssi þeir á rassinn á Öskubusku, og takið það til yðar, allt slíkt sem hjá fór þá Kolur kryppa sarð hana, og sitið í þann frið, sem þér fáið af henni. *Valete*.

> And so we end the saga of Vilmundur viðutan with this final word from him who has written it: that he who has read it out, and those who have listened to it, and all those who are not so rich that they have to pay tax to our king, can kiss Öskubuska on the arse: take for yourselves all that came when Kolur kryppa screwed her, and enjoy what friendship you can get from her. *Valete* [Farewell].

This explicit *explicit* was so provocative that, at some point, an attempt was made to erase it, and it cannot now be seen in its original form except under ultraviolet light. 343a may once have contained the very same epilogue, but we cannot be completely sure because the second half of its ending, starting from the clause invoking Öskubuska, has been erased and written over. The significance of this epilogue is that it highlights a new role on the part of the narrator: a direct, self-conscious address to the reader.[20] By invoking both the reader and a character from the already finished saga and inviting them to interact, the epilogue 'inhabits a textually and conceptually unstable space poised between the narrative world and the "real" world, in which these two worlds may momentarily meet' (O'Connor 2005, 125). However readers or audiences may have reacted, the authorial self-consciousness involved here can offer some insights into how the saga was perceived by the author of the epilogue, whether this was the relevant scribe of 586 or an earlier author of the saga (as would be the case if 343a once contained the same epilogue in its entirety). Even if we accept that the epilogue is separate from the question of fictionality in the saga proper (O'Connor 2005, 125), the fact that the characters of Kolur and Öskubuska are so cheekily deployed outside their narrative context partly subverts the gravitas of their roles within the story. The author of the epilogue clearly saw the saga as a text to be played with, and intended it to be seen as compatible with a level of imagination beyond that of the fantastic narrative—but this in turn draws attention back to the imaginative processes underpinning the narrative itself. In other words, the epilogue simultaneously acknowledges and challenges the central requirement of fiction: the cooperation of the reader's imagination.

The text of *Bósa saga* in 586 also ends with an *explicit* not found in either of the other two fifteenth-century manuscripts,[21] but it is unclear at what stage it might have been added to the saga, whether by the scribes of 586 or some earlier author. It appears as follows (on f.19r) (Jiriczek 1893, 63):

> *ok* lúku*m* vær her nu saugu Baugubosa *ok* signe þa sa*n*cta Busla alla se*m* her hafa til hlýtt lesit *ok* skrifat edr her nauckut til feingit edr gott at giort A-M-E-N.

> and here we now end the saga of Bögu-Bósi, and may Saint Busla bless everyone who has listened, read and written, or who has got something or done some good from here. Amen.

Although it is far less crude than the epilogue of *Vilmundar saga*, we find the same process in operation: the saga's formal ending is followed by a change in narratorial perspective and a sarcastic invocation of a transgressive female figure. Busla is a sorceress and Bósi's foster-mother, and

---

[20] In this sense, the epilogue is slightly reminiscent of those found in some saint's lives which conclude by invoking the name of Christ.

[21] The text in 577 simply ends with *og lukum vær nu hier saugu B[ögu]-B[ósa]* 'and here we now end the saga of Bögu-Bósi'. The text in 343a is defective, missing the ending.

her primary role in the saga is to persuade King Hringr of Gautland to reduce Bósi's death sentence after Bósi's killing of the king's bastard son. Busla's method of persuasion is to immobilise the king and threaten him with two impressively colourful curse poems, called *Buslubœn* 'Busla's Prayer' and *Syrpuvers* 'Syrpa Verse', along with a runic riddle.[22] Her only other appearance comes at the end of the saga's climactic battle, where, in dog-form, she apparently sacrifices herself to kill the enemy king. Busla is marked as a flamboyantly transgressive character not just by her ready use of magic and her ferocious verses, but also by her success in overpowering and overturning the will of King Hringr. In this latter aspect she is similar to Öskubuska, and undoubtedly much of the provocative and humorous potential of these epilogues derives from the fact that the monstrous women being invoked are subversive in action as well as nature.[23] Although Busla and Öskubuska are very different characters, their fantastical transgressive potential was clearly thought, by whoever wrote the sagas' extended epilogues, to be similar enough that they were both appropriate tools with which to break the fourth wall of the reader's imagination. Because 586 contains both epilogues, with *Bósa saga* and *Vilmundar saga* written consecutively, we do not need to answer the question of who wrote the epilogues to say with confidence that the scribes of 586 not only saw these sagas as good bookfellows, but also intended the reader to view them as such. The presence of these two epilogues reinforces the structural and thematic similarities shared by the two sagas, as well as the all-important genealogical connection that is attested by both sagas in 586 and seems to have been canonical to both traditions even if not all manuscripts of *Vilmundar saga* mention it.

2d. *Hálfdanar saga Eysteinssonar*

While *Parcevals saga* and *Bósa saga* were important influences for protagonist portrayal and development in *Vilmundar saga*, by far the greatest influence on its plot was *Hálfdanar saga Eysteinssonar*. *Hálfdanar saga* is a *fornaldarsaga* which, like *Bósa saga* and *Vilmundar saga*, most probably dates to the fourteenth century, but is only preserved in manuscripts from the fifteenth century onwards. Its earliest two extant manuscript

---

[22] For an extended discussion of these fascinating verses, see Lozzi Gallo 2004, 119–46. On the runes, see Thompson 1978, 50–56.

[23] Interestingly, the epilogue of *Vilhjálms saga sjóðs*, another romance saga, also contains a sarcastic invocation of two trollish sisters, 'blessed' Balbumba and 'sanctified' Sísigambr, as well as all other trolls mentioned in the saga (Loth 1964, 136).

witnesses are AM 586 4to and AM 343 a 4to, both of which also contain *Vilmundar saga*, as previously discussed. Finnur Jónsson (1924, 118) went so far as to call *Vilmundar saga* 'en ubetydelig saga og en stærk efterligning af Halfdan Eysteinssöns saga' 'an insignificant saga and a strong imitation of *Hálfdanar saga Eysteinssonar*'. While this is perhaps an overly dismissive assessment, the structural similarities between the two sagas are substantial:

	Hálfdanar saga Eysteinssonar	*Vilmundar saga viðutan*
1	Jarl Skúli of Álaborg (in Garðaríki) has a slave called Kolr, who is as strong as twelve men (ch. 2).	King Vísivalldur of Garðaríki is given a slave called Kolur, who is as strong as twelve men (ch. 2).
2	An invasion is imminent, with one objective being to capture Skúli's foster-daughter, Princess Ingigerðr of Aldeigjuborg (also in Garðaríki; ch. 4).	A wicked suitor arrives for Vísivalldur's daughter, Princess Sóley (ch. 4).
3	The ill Skúli enlists Kolr's help to defend the city for him. Kolr is promised Ingigerðr in marriage if successful (ch. 5).	Sóley enlists Kolur's help to kill the suitor for her. She pledges herself to him if successful (ch. 4)
4	As part of the deal, Princess Ingigerðr switches appearances with Kolr's daughter Ingigerðr, so that the princess can avoid forced marriage if things go badly (ch. 5).	Separately, Sóley summons and switches appearances with her serving-woman Öskubuska, to avoid her promised marriage to Kolur (ch. 5).
5	(see 8 below)	Sóley loses her shoe; Vilmundur finds it. He overhears her pledging marriage to the man who returns it (ch. 8).
6	The disguised Princess Ingigerðr infiltrates Hálfdan's court. While she sleeps, he removes her glove and ring and notices her beautiful hand. She takes them back, curses Hálfdan to be without peace until the same hand, glove and ring are readily given to him and then flees (ch. 8).	Vilmundur enters Öskubuska's kitchen uninvited and encounters the disguised Sóley, who attacks him. They grapple, and Vilmundur overpowers her, squeezing her hand and neck (ch. 11).
7	Ingigerðr shows Hálfdan her glove, hand and ring, as proof that they have met before (ch. 19).	Vilmundur produces Sóley's shoe, and is shown her hand (still marked by their earlier scuffle) and ring (which he is never explicitly said to have seen) as proof that they have met before (ch. 23).

| 8 | Ingigerðr gives Hálfdan her glove as a pledge of marriage (ch. 19). | (see 5 above) |
| 9 | Hálfdan and Ingigerðr marry (ch. 21). | Vilmundur and Sóley marry (ch. 24). |

Although each hero has different adventures between his encounter with the disguised princess (no. 6 above) and his eventual reunion with her (no. 7), it is clear that their character trajectories are parallel for substantial sections of their sagas.

Apart from structural similarities, we also find superficial similarities between the two sagas. The table above demonstrates that certain character functions and actions in *Hálfdanar saga* find parallels in *Vilmundar saga*, and to this we might also note that the names of three characters in *Vilmundar saga* correspond to those of characters from *Hálfdanar saga*. The first is demonstrated in the table above: each saga features a servant called Kolr/Kolur, who is promised the princess's hand in marriage in exchange for his help against a foreign threat. The second pair of characters with corresponding names is Úlfr inn illi 'the Evil', a minor villain named in chapter 1 of *Hálfdanar saga*, and Úlfur illt-eitt 'Only Evil', Sóley's suitor in chapter 4 of *Vilmundar saga* who is quickly killed off. The third pair of corresponding names belongs in fact to the same character appearing in both sagas: Sviði inn sókndjarfi, ally of Hálfdan in *Hálfdanar saga*, and Sviði, the father of Vilmundur and son of Bósi in *Vilmundar saga* (and *Bósa saga*).

The second superficial similarity is that each saga includes a significant amount of action set in Garðaríki. Connections between continental Scandinavia and Garðaríki are mentioned in the *konungasögur* (Shafer 2009, 141–44), as well as in many *fornaldarsögur*, namely *Hálfdanar saga Eysteinssonar*, *Hervarar saga ok Heiðreks*, *Hrólfs saga Gautrekssonar*, *Göngu-Hrólfs saga*, *Sturlaugs saga starfsama*, *Yngvars saga víðförla* and *Örvar-Odds saga*. Garðaríki also features in three other borderline *fornaldarsögur*, *Hrings saga ok Tryggva*, *Sigrgarðs saga frækna* and *Þjalar-Jóns saga*.

It has already been suggested in Section 1 that Garðaríki in Old Norse literature represents a space both northern and non-Scandinavian. With this unique position, familiar yet distant, we find a set of associations that is strikingly consistent across the fantastical sagas that use it as a location. Evidence for this can be found in the recurring use of the name Ingigerðr. The historical Princess Ingigerðr of Sweden (1010–50) was the daughter of King Óláfr Skötkonungr (also known in Norse texts as Óláfr sænski 'the Swedish') and the wife of Yaroslav I of Novgorod (Old Norse

Jarizleifr).[24] In Old Norse literature the name is, with two very minor exceptions, only ever used either for the historical Princess Ingigerðr Óláfsdóttir (in historical sagas), or, in fantastic sagas, as the name of a fictional princess of an eastern kingdom, usually Garðaríki or a city within it.[25] In *Hálfdanar saga Eysteinssonar* in particular, Princess Ingigerðr is specifically associated with the city of Aldeigjuborg (Staraya Ladoga), which the historical princess notably secured from Yaroslav as part of her dowry, as is recounted in *Óláfs saga helga* (Bjarni Aðalbjarnarson 1945, 147). The rare and specific use of the name Ingigerðr in *fornaldarsögur* demonstrates that Garðaríki as a geographical texture was intended to evoke a consistent sense of veracity through historically based familiarity, as a backdrop against which each saga presents the narrative of its legendary history.

Although *Vilmundar saga* contains no Ingigerðr, this same process of a shared association between historical name and geographical space is still at work. Vísivalldur, the king of Garðaríki in *Vilmundar saga*, is probably named after the historical Vísivaldr Jarizleifsson (Olsson 1949, xix), that is, Grand Prince Vsevolod I of Kiev (1030–93), son of the aforementioned Yaroslav and Ingigerðr Óláfsdóttir. Apart from *Vilmundar saga*, the name features in Old Norse literature only as the name of this historical monarch.[26] The effect of the name *Vísivalldur* is very much the same as the

---

[24] A fuller discussion of the historical Yaroslav and Ingigerðr in Norse and Russian sources may be found in Cross 1929.

[25] In the *fornaldarsögur*, we find characters named Ingigerðr in *Göngu-Hrólfs saga* (as a princess of Garðaríki); *Hálfdanar saga Eysteinssonar* (shared by a princess of Aldeigjuborg in Garðaríki, and the servant with whom the princess switches appearances); *Sturlaugs saga starfsama* (as a princess of Garðaríki) and the pseudo-historical *Yngvars saga víðförla* (as the historical Ingigerðr Óláfsdóttir). In the borderline *fornaldarsaga Sigrgarðs saga frækna*, there is also a Princess Ingigerðr whose domain is not Garðaríki (which does feature in the saga), but Tartaría, or the fantastical far-eastern kingdom of Tartary (Hall et al. 2013, 101–02). The two exceptions are the princess's namesake and *doppelgänger* in *Hálfdanar saga* (the only Ingigerðr who is not royal), and the fictionalised queen of Sweden in *Hrólfs saga Gautrekssonar* (whose Swedish connection is still consistent with the directed use of the name). See Aðalheiður Guðmundsdóttir 2009 for a brief discussion on the historical Ingigerðr and her connection to *Göngu-Hrólfs saga*, *Hálfdanar saga* and *Yngvars saga*.

[26] The historical Vísivaldr is named in *Óláfs saga Tryggvasonar*, the Old Norse translation of Oddr Snorrason's twelfth-century Latin biography of King Óláfr Tryggvason (Ólafur Halldórsson 2006, 226), as well as in Snorri Sturluson's *Óláfs saga helga* (Bjarni Aðalbjarnarson 1945, 436).

use of the name Ingigerðr in *Hálfdanar saga* and other *fornaldarsögur*: it serves to situate the narrative in a universe that is at once literary and veracious, as well as ultimately familiar to the reader of fantastic sagas. Indeed, the depiction of a king named Vísivalldur as an offshoot of the convention of princesses named Ingigerðr in *fornaldarsögur* reinforces the idea of *Vilmundar saga* as a Russian-based spin-off of Scandinavian-based romances.

Owing to its location along the *austrvegr* (the 'Eastern Way', or the naval route east of Scandinavia through the Baltic) Garðaríki is also consistently represented in saga literature as a 'gateway to the East', whether to Constantinople or Syria or some other far-eastern kingdom (Sverrir Jakobsson 2006, 937–41). In analysing the *austrvegr* in the 'widely-travelled' *fornaldarsögur*, namely *Örvar-Odds saga*, *Yngvars saga víðförla* and *Eiríks saga víðförla*, Sverrir Jakobsson highlighted several consistent aspects associated with the *austrvegr* in those texts. One such aspect was that 'the "Eastern Road" was not only a progress towards a geographical goal, it also led to social and spiritual advancement' (2006, 942). Although Sverrir's discussion did not include legendary romance *fornaldarsögur*, the association of the theme of social advancement with the eastern lands beyond Scandinavia is strikingly consistent in these texts as well, not least because such protagonistic progression is intrinsic to romance. Yet there is a specific way in which *Hálfdanar saga Eysteinssonar* and *Vilmundar saga* express social advancement which cannot simply be attributed to the generic demands of romance. In these two sagas, as well as in another legendary romance mostly based in Russia, *Egils saga einhenda ok Ásmundar berserkjabana*, social advancement is manifested through the same motif complex. Each of the saga heroes, Egill, Hálfdan and Vilmundur, is presented with a hand and a ring which they had once encountered, and his recognition of these tokens leads directly to a newfound alliance resulting in marriage and the hero's rehabilitation into society from a position of exile.

	Hálfdanar saga Eysteinssonar	*Vilmundar saga viðutan*	*Egils saga einhenda*
Loss of ring	Hálfdan removes the disguised Ingigerðr's glove and ring and notices her beautiful hand. She takes them back and flees (ch. 8).	Vilmundur and the disguised Sóley grapple, and he leaves a mark on her hand (ch. 11).	Egill's arm, with his ring, is said to have been chopped off while he is helping a *flagðkona* resist a bully of a *jötunn* (ch. 11).

Exile (not necessarily linked to loss of ring)	Hálfdan has a series of solo adventures in a forest (chs 16–18).	Vilmundur is exiled by the king (ch. 18).	Egill becomes a raider (ch. 3; he does not return home until ch. 17).
Return of the ring	Hálfdan arrives in Kirjálabotn (Karelia) in the east. To win his help against imminent invasion, Ingigerðr shows Hálfdan her glove, hand and ring, as proof that they have met before (ch. 19).	Vilmundur arrives at Silven's house-in-a-stone. Silven shows Vilmundur Sóley's marked hand, with her (previously unmentioned) ring, as proof that they have met before (ch. 23).	Egill is in Jötunheimar in the north. The *flagðkona* Skinnefja had found and preserved Egill's arm and ring, and shows them to him as proof that they have met before. She reattaches his arm (ch. 14).
Resolution	Hálfdan helps Ingigerðr defeat his evil ex-ally Úlfkell. He is reconciled with Ingigerðr and marries her (chs 20–21).	Vilmundur brings the real Sóley back to her father, is reconciled with him and marries Sóley (chs 23–24).	Allied with Skinnefja, Egill and Ásmundr rescue the two Russian princesses from the *jötnar* and eventually marry them (chs 16–17).

The similarities shown in the above table are compounded by geographical consistency. All three heroes are ultimately of Scandinavian origin (Vilmundur distantly so). Russia is a key location in all three sagas.[27] In each case, the recognition of the hand and ring occurs in a place of otherness, away from society. This is important because it represents the foreign space where the hero must prove his worth (or where he has already proved his worth, in the case of Vilmundur), by accomplishing a quest in aid of a Russian royal figure. Each of the three heroes is then rewarded with marriage to a princess—in each case a Russian princess. That the heroes' social advancement should be achieved specifically through service to eastern royalty is significant, because this was another feature

---

[27] *Egils saga einhenda* opens by noting that its setting, Rússía, is a kingdom bordering Garðaríki (Lagerholm 1927, 1–2). However, according to the encyclopaedic first section of the part of Hauksbók preserved in the early fourteenth-century AM 544 4to, Garðaríki is in fact just the Norse name for the same kingdom (Finnur Jónsson and Eiríkur Jónsson 1892–96, 155). In any case, a similar setting is intended to be evoked.

identified by Sverrir Jakobsson with reference to the 'widely-travelled' *fornaldarsögur* (2006, 937–39). From this shared motif complex, we can see that the relationship discussed by Sverrir between the *austrvegr* (including Garðaríki) and the theme of social advancement is expressed consistently across these three legendary romances. The fact that *Hálfdanar saga* and *Vilmundar saga* share this geographic texture, along with its usual associations, strengthens the more specific similarities between them that we have seen, and is a testament to the depth of the relationship between the two sagas.

The significance of Garðaríki as a location with a set of common associations can be seen not just in literary parallels, but also in the compilation of one particular medieval manuscript: AM 343 a 4to. Sverrir Jakobsson highlights the peculiar fact that *Yngvars saga víðförla*, a semi-historical *fornaldarsaga* featuring a version of Garðaríki with its historical ruler Yaroslav I, appears in the same medieval manuscript as a redaction of *Örvar-Odds saga* in which 'the position of Garðaríki is very much enhanced' (2006, 938). This manuscript co-occurrence, he notes, is made even more striking by the fact that 'both protagonists enter into a relationship with a royal lady named Silkisif (the name might be construed as an onomatopoeic near-equivalent of the Old Slavonic *Ellisif–Elizaveta*)', and that Örvar-Oddr's encounter with Silkisif takes place in Garðaríki and not in Húnaland as in the earlier redaction of the saga (Sverrir Jakobsson 2006, 939). However, *Yngvars saga* and *Örvar-Odds saga* are not the only two sagas in 343a with significant narrative interest in Garðaríki and the near-East region outside Scandinavia. The manuscript also contains *Egils saga einhenda*, *Hálfdanar saga Eysteinssonar* and *Vilmundar saga*. The latter two are based in Garðaríki, while *Egils saga einhenda* is based in *Rússía*. This strongly suggests that geographical clustering was a factor in the compilation of 343a, especially since the manuscript also contains all four Hrafnista sagas (*Ketils saga hængs*, *Gríms saga loðinkinna*, *Örvar-Odds saga* and *Áns saga bogsveigis*),[28] as well as three sagas which involve the semi-mythical kingdom of Glæsisvellir, a kingdom often portrayed as a gateway to a kingdom of *jötnar* (*Þorsteins þáttr bæjarmagns*, *Samsons saga fagra* and *Bósa saga*; on Glæsisvellir see Tolkien 1960, 84–86 and Simek 1986). It therefore seems that for the compiler of 343a, *Vilmundar saga*'s setting alone may have been a crucial factor in its inclusion, notwithstanding the set of common associations attached to it.

---

[28] 343a is in fact the only extant medieval manuscript to contain *Áns saga* alongside the other three Hrafnista sagas.

2e. *Eskja and the Transmission of Cinderella in Old Norse Literature*[29]

The final source to be introduced, *Eskja*, must necessarily be included in a wider discussion of the transmission of the Cinderella tale type in Old Norse literature. This section will therefore be prefaced by a broader introduction to the tale type, including an episodic breakdown of its general structure that will be applied to all the Cinderella variants identified here. Detailed treatment of *Vilmundar saga*'s elements of Cinderella-related interest will also be provided, in order to situate the saga properly within the transmission of the tale type both in the context of Old Norse literature and in a global context.

The Cinderella tale type is an ancient and international one, stretching back over two millennia across many different literary and cultural contexts. The earliest known literary variant seems to be the tale of Rhodopis in book 17 of Strabo's *Geographica*, written in the first century BC (Radt 2005, 464); the same tale is also found in book 13 of Aelian's *Varia Historia* in the third century AD (Wilson 1997, 442–43). Other early Cinderella variants include the tale of Aspasia, also found in Aelian (Wilson 1997, 342–59; Anderson 2000, 29–33); the sixth-century Hellenistic *Joseph and Asenath* (Anderson 2000, 33–37); and the Chinese tale of Ye Xian in the late Tang collection *Youyang Zazu* (The Youyang Miscellany), written down by Duan Chengshi around 850–60 AD (Waley 1947, 226–38). In addition to these, partial traces of the tale type can be found in a variety of early stories from different cultures and genres. Graham Anderson (2010, 38–41) has shown that elements of the tale survive in Greek and Sumerian mythology, and concluded that the tale had been reworked in different generic contexts by classical antiquity 'as fairytale and as romance, and perhaps even as myth as well' (38–39). Juliana Dresvina has also identified Cinderella resonances in the Old and Middle English lives of St Margaret of Antioch (Dresvina 2009; 2016, 193–201).

However, Rhodopis and her fellow ancient Cinderellas are hardly household names today. The majority of Cinderella research tends to focus on modern variants, beginning with two early modern tales: Giambattista Basile's 'La Gatta cenerentola' 'The Ashy Cat' (published posthumously in 1634–36 in his *Lo cunto de li cunti* 'The tale of tales') and Charles Perrault's 'Cendrillon' (published in 1697 in his *Histoires ou contes du temps passé* 'Stories or tales of past times'). Also widely familiar to Cinderella scholars and enthusiasts is the Grimm Brothers' 'Aschenputtel', a tale

---

[29] Along with portions of the previous sections, this section is derived from my article published in *Folklore* on 21 December 2018, available online: https://www.tandfonline.com/doi/10.1080/0015587X.2018.1515207. I am grateful to the editor, Dr Jessica Hemming, for permission to reproduce this material.

which underwent some evolution between the first and seventh editions of the brothers' *Kinder- und Hausmärchen* 'Children's and Household Tales' in 1812 and 1857 respectively. However, it was Perrault's variant that became the quintessential and universally recognised Cinderella tale through the subsequent centuries. Indeed, even before Disney adapted it into their classic 1950 animated film, Stith Thompson noted (1946, 127) that Perrault's version had already become synecdochal for the Cinderella tradition as a whole:

> The version of Perrault is so familiar through two hundred and fifty years' use as a nursery tale that we are likely to think that all the details he mentions are essential. Some of them, as a matter of fact, are practically unknown elsewhere.

Thompson's observation draws attention to a basic but important point; namely that it is not individual 'details' that define a folktale variant, but rather the broader narrative structure. According to the Aarne-Thompson-Uther folktale classification system, the general structure of the Cinderella tale type (ATU 510A) is as follows (Uther 2004, 1:293–95):

1. The Persecuted Heroine
2. Magic Help
3. Meeting the Prince
4. Proof of Identity
5. Marriage with the Prince

Probably the most universally recognised episode in the Cinderella tale structure is the Proof of Identity, which is often famously manifested through the iconic bridal shoe. Cinderella's shoe is 'perhaps the most salient feature of Cinderella proper' (Cox 1892, xl), and it is undoubtedly one of the best-known fairy-tale motifs today. In Stith Thompson's *Motif-Index* this motif is classified as H36.1, 'slipper test' or 'shoe test', and involves the heroine's identity being proven through the confirmation that a certain shoe, which she had previously lost, must exclusively belong to her. However, not all Cinderella variants have the heroine's identity tested by a shoe; indeed, of the ancient variants listed above, only Rhodopis and Ye Xian contain the shoe. It goes without saying that tales containing a lost-and-found shoe are much easier to identify as ATU 510A variants than tales which follow the tale type's overall structure but lack the shoe. With this in mind, it will be helpful first to outline *Vilmundar saga*'s adherence to the Cinderella structure outlined above, as the presence of a bridal shoe in the saga makes it a useful starting point, and indeed reference point, for the discussion.

Behind the trappings of a medieval Icelandic legendary romance, the narrative spine of *Vilmundar saga* is that of the Cinderella folktale. This combination should not be regarded as especially peculiar, given the generic flexibility within the early Cinderella tale as demonstrated by Anderson, and particularly the early precedent of a romance-like reworking in the form of Aelian's Aspasia (Anderson 2000, 29–33). The adherence of *Vilmundar saga* to ATU 510A's structure can be seen below:

'Cinderella' episode	Manifestation in *Vilmundar saga viðutan*
1. Persecution	Sóley is said to be favoured less than her twin sister. She is also fostered outside the royal court, unlike her sister.
2. Aid	After her change of identity, she occasionally meets with her only confidantes, her foster-mother and foster-sister, in a (house-in-a-)stone.
3. Meeting the Prince	In disguise, she meets Vilmundur in the royal kitchen. She grapples with him, and he leaves a mark on her hand before leaving.
4. Proof of Identity	She has earlier lost her shoe, pledging to marry the man who returns it. Vilmundur has found her shoe, and later returns it. Vilmundur recognises her eyes and the mark he left on her hand during their earlier meeting.
5. Marriage with the Prince	Sóley and Vilmundur marry.

Beyond *Vilmundar saga*'s structural adherence to the tale type, it also contains a number of motifs commonly found in Cinderella variants. As stated, the lost-and-found shoe is by far the most familiar, and in this case it is clearly a borrowing because the condition that Sóley must walk around with one bare foot until her shoe is returned—which invites the possibility of a 'perfect fit' function—is never given any more narrative attention. The saga also contains a persecuted heroine motif which is notable for being awkwardly manifested, as will be fully discussed presently. Another motif of interest is the house-in-a-stone in which Sóley meets with her confidantes. This does not seem to be based on the stones inhabited by dwarfs in roughly contemporary *fornaldarsögur* and *riddarasögur*; the house-in-a-stone is not reminiscent of these in either function or depiction. Instead, this is probably an example of the 'treasure stone' motif (Einar Sigurðsson 1962, 81, n. 1). Anna Birgitta Rooth (1980, 101) noted the treasure stone motif to be an exclusively northern European version of the 'treasure tree' motif found in some Cinderella variants, in which a tree supplies clothes, food or some other type of aid to the heroine. Although the house-in-a-stone provides no specific aid to Sóley, it has the implied function of a shelter, as it is the only friendly space for Sóley after her change of identity. The northern European localisation of the treasure stone motif fits *Vilmundar saga* perfectly, and the saga seems to be the earliest attestation of this motif, making the late fourteenth century the latest possible date for its development (Einar Sigurðsson 1962, 81, n. 1).

The first thing to note when considering the persecuted heroine element in *Vilmundar saga* is that the very biographical configuration of the Cinderella figure in Sóley is peculiar in its literary context, for the reason that twin sisters are exceedingly rare in Old Norse literature. Indeed, biological twins are quite rare in medieval European romance in general (Larrington 2015, 60–61).[30] The dramatic potential of twins is obvious: mistaken or substituted identity is a well-established source of dramatic tension, with prime examples including Shakespeare's *Comedy of Errors* and *Twelfth Night*. In *Vilmundar saga*, however, Sóley and Gullbrá are never in direct competition with each other. Not once do they even interact within the narrative. Their paths only cross at their birth and at the saga's resolution; Sóley only mentions Gullbrá once, as part of her reporting of news from the city; and there are very few characters with whom both sisters interact. The utter triviality of their sibling relationship seems to reflect a blind version of a motif that was functional in a source from which *Vilmundar saga* borrowed.

2e.i. *Eskja*

The source in question was probably *Eskja* 'Ash-tree'. *Eskja* is a tale in the compilation known as *Strengleikar* 'Stringed instruments', which consists of Norse prose translations of the *lais* of Marie de France. These twelfth-century lays (long narrative literary ballads) were translated from Old French into the Old Norse *Strengleikar* in the thirteenth century at the court of King Hákon Hákonarson of Norway (Cook and Tveitane 1979, xiv–xviii). *Eskja* is a translation of the *lai* called *Le Fresne* 'The ash-tree', and it is faithful to its Old French source in substance.

In *Le Fresne*/*Eskja* a noblewoman finds herself in a bind when she gives birth to twin daughters, having earlier suggested that another woman's set

---

[30] It is worth mentioning that in medieval European literature the plot devices associated with twinning did not always involve biological twins. The widespread tale of 'Amicus and Amelius', which exists in numerous versions from across medieval Europe, including one in Old Norse, and which is itself classified as ATU 516C (and is related to ATU 303, 'The Twin Brothers'), is a prominent example of dual protagonists of identical appearance who might be regarded as symbolic twins, but were not born to the same parents.

of twins was a sign of infidelity. Her handmaiden helps her abandon one of her twins under an ash-tree by an abbey, with nothing but the beautiful cloth in which the baby is wrapped, and a ring to help the child by serving as proof of her original social status. The child is raised in the abbey and is named after the ash-tree (OF *fresne*, ON *eskja*).[31] When she has grown up, she meets a knight called Gurun at the abbey, and they fall in love. However, Gurun is advised to marry a noblewoman instead, and eventually he agrees to marry a woman who happens to be the heroine's sister, and is named after the hazel-tree (OF *coudre*, ON *hesla*).[32] On the wedding night the mother of the twins recognises the beautiful cloth belonging to the heroine, and the ring then confirms her identity. Her noble lineage is thus revealed to all. With general approval, Gurun divorces La Coudre/Hesla the following day and marries Le Fresne/Eskja—and the story completes its resolution with the rather perfunctory note of La Coudre/Hesla's marriage to an unnamed nobleman.

It is clear from the storyline that *Le Fresne*/*Eskja* is also a Cinderella variant.[33] *Eskja* has never before been formally identified as such, but *Le Fresne* has (Anderson 2000, 41–42; the *lai*'s general affinity with aspects of the Cinderella tale was previously noted in Shippey 1988, 76–77). Its faithful Norse translation is therefore a variant. It adheres to the tale type structure as follows:

'Cinderella' episode	Manifestation in *Le Fresne*/*Eskja*
1. Persecution	The heroine is exposed as a baby.
2. Aid	She receives shelter from an ash-tree.
3. Meeting the Prince	She meets Gurun at the abbey and enters a romantic relationship with him, but it is broken off because of their differing social classes.
4. Proof of Identity	She proves her identity and accompanying nobility through possession of a beautiful cloth and ring which had been left with her.
5. Marriage with the Prince	She marries the knight.

In the scanty scholarship that exists on *Vilmundar saga*, *Eskja* has never previously been recognised as a source for the saga. However, it is apparent

---

[31] The name Eskja is 'a feminine coinage based on *askr* [ash (tree)]' (Cook and Tveitane 1979, 50, n. 2).

[32] The name Hesla is 'a feminine coinage based on *hasl* [hazel]' (Cook and Tveitane 1979, 56, n. 1). The contrast between the fertile hazel and the barren ash is raised in both the French poem and the Norse prose translation.

[33] The plot will also be familiar as a form of the Griselda tale (ATU 887) that appears in Boccaccio's *Decameron*, Petrarch's *De obedientia ac fide uxoria mythologia* and Chaucer's *Clerk's Tale*.

that their narrative arrangements are very similar. Each contains twin sisters of noble birth, one of whom is forced away in secret, undergoes a change of identity and becomes a commoner, while the other is little more than a plot device. In neither narrative do the sisters openly interact; they follow divergent paths and do not even occupy the same space at any point between their birth and the resolution. In both stories this resolution is provided by the eventual return of the exiled sister and the revelation of her identity. Not only does each narrative have a pair of twin sisters, then, but both pairs follow identically divergent narrative trajectories. The duplication of this formula alone is suggestive of influence. To add to this, there are two important elements that are active in *Eskja* but present and redundant in *Vilmundar saga*.

First, in *Eskja*, the persecuted heroine motif is somewhat muted because of the lack of both sibling jealousy and a reason for the mother-figure's specific persecution of the heroine over anyone else (Eskja is arbitrarily chosen for abandonment). Nonetheless, the mother's specific choice of one twin over the other demonstrates that some of the substance of the motif remains. In *Vilmundar saga*, Sóley is mentioned by the narrator to be the less favoured of the two sisters (*kongur unni henni minna, en þó voru þær systur báðar vinsælar* 'the king loved her less than her sister, but both sisters were still popular'), and she is raised outside the royal court, in the loving fosterage of Silven, but at no point in the saga is she persecuted or mistreated by any member of her family. Even with the marriage proposal of Úlfur illt-eitt—the event that causes Sóley to flee home and triggers the main dramatic dissonance of the saga—her father expressly states that the decision over the suit is up to Sóley herself. Yet we can be fairly certain that Sóley was intended to fill the role of the persecuted heroine because there are traces of two figures who usually accompany it in European Cinderella tales: the wicked mother or stepmother and the rival sibling or step-sibling (Rooth 1951, 98; these two motifs are respectively denoted S31 and L55 in Thompson's *Motif-Index*). Silven assumes a parental role after the death of Sóley's own mother, and Silven's own daughter is technically Sóley's foster-sister, although this latter relationship is never explicitly mentioned. However, neither character is remotely antagonistic. Silven is certainly not wicked, as her main function throughout the saga is to support and advise Sóley.[34] Silven's daughter is neither wicked nor important; her only role in the story is to be held responsible by her mother, rather inexplicably, for Sóley's lost shoe. Her sheer insignificance is reflected

---

[34] The wicked stepmother would certainly not have been out of place in an Icelandic legendary romance; a prominent example can be found in the figure of Lúða in *Hjálmþés saga ok Ölvis*, which is roughly contemporary with *Vilmundar saga*.

in the fact that she is the only recurring individual in the saga never to be named. Thus, although *Vilmundar saga* contains all the potential of the familiar 'Cinderella' arrangement of persecuted heroine, wicked (step-)mother and rival (step-)sibling, it suppresses their usual functions to the extent that only their basic family relationships survive.

The second element that is active in *Eskja* but present and redundant in *Vilmundar saga* is sisterly competition. Eskja's status as a twin leads to a form of substitution of the sisters' identities, with both twins becoming unknowing competitors for Gurun's hand in marriage. Like the persecuted heroine motif, this motif is also muted in *Eskja*, as neither sister displays any competitive intent (or even awareness of the other's existence), and, in the logic of the story, the romantic triangle involving the twins comes about as pure coincidence (and partly because the cast of characters is small). In *Vilmundar saga* there is no sisterly competition at all. As outlined above, the two sisters do not interact with each other, and there are few characters with whom both of them interact. The character with the most substantial interactions with both sisters is Vilmundur, Sóley's eventual husband, but even though he spends a night in Gullbrá's tower, the saga offers no hint of a romantic triangle. The fact that the two elements detailed above are present (albeit muted) in *Eskja* and present but non-functional in *Vilmundar saga* is telling, because it demonstrates a further depth to the probable influence of the former on the latter, extending beyond their shared narrative configuration and trajectory of the heroine.

Eskja seems to be the earliest Cinderella tale in the Old Norse language, and, despite the nuanced similarities in the trajectory of their heroines' careers, it will be noticed that *Eskja* is fundamentally a distinctly different Cinderella tale from *Vilmundar saga*, not least because the two stories deploy different allomotifs in some cases. For instance, in *Eskja*, the motif of Meeting the Prince is located not in the kitchen but at a church (a reasonably common motif in European Cinderella tales; cf. Rooth 1980, 115), and the infant heroine's shelter under the ash-tree, whose significance is crystallised in the heroine's own name, is clearly a straightforward example of the treasure tree motif, whereas *Vilmundar saga* deploys an entirely different allomotif, namely the treasure stone variant. Most notably, the Proof of Identity episode is structured substantially differently in the two stories; not only does *Eskja* lack the iconic lost-and-found shoe, but the Proof of Identity is also established through items (including a piece of cloth) that had been intentionally left with the infant heroine in her abandonment, not through items which she had misplaced. As a result, Le Fresne/Eskja's identity is proven not to her future husband but to her mother.

The fact that *Eskja* is Norwegian and not Icelandic highlights a minor caveat that must be kept in mind when assessing the influence of *Eskja*—or any of the *Strengleikar* texts—on medieval Icelandic literature; namely that we have no known and extant medieval Icelandic manuscripts containing any of the *Strengleikar* (Aðalheiður Guðmundsdóttir 2014, 120–22). However, Aðalheiður Guðmundsdóttir has noted that although manuscript evidence is lacking, there is potential literary evidence that *Eskja* was already known in Iceland in the thirteenth century. This literary evidence can be found in the thirteenth-century *fornaldarsaga*, *Ragnars saga loðbrókar*.

2e.ii. *Ragnars saga*

Ragnars saga details the legendary career of Ragnarr loðbrók, one of the most famous heroes of medieval Scandinavia. The saga is just one of a number of sources, medieval and post-medieval, historical and literary, which deal with this figure (McTurk 1991, 53–62). Among the feats of Ragnarr and his sons, the saga tells of Ragnarr's courtship of and marriage to his second wife, Kráka, who seems to Ragnarr and his men to be a common-born woman, but whom the narrative has already revealed to be Áslaug, orphaned daughter of the legendary Sigurðr Fáfnisbani and Brynhildr Buðladóttir, of *Völsunga saga* fame. The biographical formula of Áslaug as depicted in *Ragnars saga*, Aðalheiður Guðmundsdóttir has argued, strongly parallels that of Eskja, to the extent that influence from *Eskja* on *Ragnars saga* must be posited. She notes

> an interesting resemblance between *Eskju ljóð* and *Ragnars saga loðbrókar* from the thirteenth century. Both tell of a highborn woman who is engaged or married to a man of high social status. The man, however, does not know about the noble origin of his fiancée/wife, and his men urge him to find himself another wife who is his equal. In the end the man is told about the woman's noble parents and decides to keep her (Aðalheiður Guðmundsdóttir 2014, 125).[35]

The specificity of this formula is important. In a wider literary context, it dramatically increases the likelihood that the story of *Le Fresne/Eskja* was already known in Iceland in the thirteenth century, adding to the plausibility of its influence on *Vilmundar saga*. In a text-specific context, it shows that *Ragnars saga* closely parallels *Eskja* in the motivations and dynamics which underpin the relationship at the centre of the second half

---

[35] As Aðalheiður notes, Rory McTurk had previously spotted an indirect connection between *Le Fresne* (rather than *Eskja*) and an Icelandic text, this time *Geirmundar þáttr heljarskinns* (McTurk 1997; cf. Aðalheiður Guðmundsdóttir 2014, 125).

of the latter's Cinderella structure (from Meeting the Prince onwards). In fact, *Ragnars saga* had also previously been identified as a Cinderella tale back in 1893, in the introduction to Marian Roalfe Cox's extraordinary collection of Cinderella variants (Cox 1893, xxxvii):

> For instance, we recognise our heroine under one of her many disguises in the story of Crow, the maiden of mean attire and low estate, who in the end turns out to be Aslaug, a princess, daughter of Sigfred and Brunhild.

Cox goes on to summarise Áslaug's career, finding the Cinderella parallels so obvious that she considers it 'unnecessary to point out the striking parallels which the above narrative presents to the common incidents of the folk-tale' (xl). For the sake of clarity, we can fit it to ATU 510A's structure as below:

'Cinderella' episode	Manifestation in *Ragnars saga loðbrókar*
2. Aid	Orphaned Áslaug receives aid from her foster-grandfather, including a paranormal source of food (a *vínlaukr* 'wine-leek').
1. Persecution	A peasant couple kill the foster-grandfather and find Áslaug, adopting her. They dress her poorly and make her do dirty housework.
3. Meeting the Prince	She meets King Ragnarr loðbrók and marries him, but he is later advised to separate from her and marry a princess instead.
4. Proof of Identity	She proves her nobility by giving birth to a son with a snake-mark in his eye, demonstrating her descent from Sigurðr Fafnisbani.
5. Marriage with the Prince	Ragnarr decides not to separate from her.

In this case the Aid and Persecution episodes are reversed, but their manifestations contain allomotifs common to many other Cinderella variants, most notably the paranormal source of food and the heroine's household chores, neither of which *Ragnars saga* derived from *Eskja*. There is also a slight variation to the Marriage with the Prince, in that Ragnarr and Áslaug are already married, but it is clear that their renewed relationship (that is, Ragnarr reaffirming his commitment to her) is a direct result of the Proof of Identity, as we would expect of a Cinderella variant. Furthermore, Ragnarr's discovery of Áslaug's noble parentage corresponds to Gurun's discovery of Le Fresne/Eskja's noble parentage, and in the latter case, this discovery actually leads to marriage. This further suggests that Ragnarr's decision not to separate from Áslaug in fact corresponds to the episode of the Marriage with the Prince, albeit modified because of the necessity of biographical circumstances. The general adherence of *Ragnars saga* to the Cinderella tale type would therefore seem to make it the second-earliest extant Cinderella variant in the Old Norse language, and the first from Iceland. Here, as in *Vilmundar saga*, the trajectory of at least part of the heroine's career was influenced by *Eskja*.

The persecuted heroines of *Eskja* and *Ragnars saga* are important features of their correspondence with ATU 510A, but neither tale contains any semblance of a Cinderella shoe. *Vilmundar saga* is in fact the earliest extant Scandinavian source for such a shoe, so this particular allomotif must either have come from a lost literary source or from an oral source. What this means is that there must have been a second Cinderella tale or tradition that influenced *Vilmundar saga*, and its identity test must have involved a shoe. Although that source no longer survives, we can glean some circumstantial information about it from *Hálfdanar saga Eysteinssonar*, which contains a close form of the motif.

2e.iii. *Hálfdanar saga Eysteinssonar*

The close structural parallels between *Hálfdanar saga Eysteinssonar* and *Vilmundar saga viðutan* have already been outlined in Section 2d above, particularly in the table on pp. xxii–xxiii. Within that table, it will be recognised that nos 5 to 9 represent Cinderella episodes: no. 6 is the Meeting with the Prince; no. 7 is the Proof of Identity episode, in both cases involving a lost-and-found garment which is set up as a pledge of marriage in no. 5/8; and no. 9 is the Marriage with the Prince. The earlier parallels between the narratives (nos 1 to 4) have no obvious connection to the Cinderella tale type, but are nonetheless crucial in establishing the structure of the dramatic trajectory of each saga. In fact, the parallels between the two sagas in nos 1 to 4 are closer than those in nos 5 to 9. Not only do we find the two sagas sharing basic details such as geographical location and the name of the male slave, but also critical episodes of the narrative formula: in both cases, the princess is promised in marriage to the slave (no. 3), but she switches appearances with a female servant (no. 4), and this secret exchange of identity remains a source of prolonged dramatic tension in both sagas. What this means is that the use of a garment as proof of identity in *Vilmundar saga* represents only a part of *Hálfdanar saga*'s enormous influence on it.

Hálfdanar saga's resonance with the Cinderella tale type was noted by Franz Rolf Schröder in his edition of the saga (Schröder 1917, 27–28), but, as is the case with *Vilmundar saga*, its Cinderella connection has not yet received the attention it deserves. We may partially redress this by assessing it according to the tale type's structure (with ambiguous manifestations placed in parentheses):

'Cinderella' episode	Manifestation in *Hálfdanar saga Eysteinssonar*
1. Persecution	(Princess Ingigerðr is orphaned by an invasion, but she herself escapes a forced marriage.)
2. Aid	(With the aid of her disguised foster-father Skúli, the disguised Ingigerðr infiltrates Hálfdan's court to avenge her father.)
3. Meeting the Prince	While she sleeps, Hálfdan removes the disguised Ingigerðr's glove and ring and notices her beautiful hand. She takes them back, curses him to be without peace until the same hand, glove and ring are readily given to him, and then flees.
4. Proof of Identity	Later in the saga, she proves her identity by showing him the glove, ring and hand that he had seen at their previous meeting, and then gives him the glove as a pledge of marriage.
5. Marriage with the Prince	Ingigerðr and Hálfdan marry.

Although this use of a garment as a proof of identity, in combination with the evidence of the closely related *Vilmundar saga*, indicates a Cinderella connection, *Hálfdanar saga* contains no especially clear Persecution and Aid episodes. Put another way, the saga's strongest candidates for Ingigerðr's Persecution and Aid episodes are manifested quite differently from how they usually appear in Cinderella variants; Ingigerðr receives no targeted ill treatment from any relatives, nor does she receive any specific form of aid beyond her foster-father Skúli's general (albeit significant) assistance. Nonetheless, the saga's versions of the themes of persecution and aid still ensure a structural progression similar to that in many Cinderella tales: the heroine suffers a loss of status as the result of an upheaval in the family structure, with only a single source of aid to rely on.

Hálfdanar saga shows no obvious influence from *Eskja*, and it has only a minor relationship with *Ragnars saga*. This relationship is relatively superficial, existing not in terms of the borrowing and adaptation of motifs, but in the creation of a simple referential relationship. This is manifested in two ways: through two genealogical relationships and a textual relationship. The first genealogical relationship is established at the beginning of the saga, through the narrator's assertion that Hálfdan's maternal great-grandfather was Sigurðr ormr-í-auga (Guðni Jónsson

1954, IV 247), who is established in *Ragnars saga* as a son of Ragnarr (Guðni Jónsson 1954, I 245–47). The claim of characters' descent from Ragnarr or his children is not especially unusual in saga literature, and it is also found in the *Íslendingasögur*. The second genealogical relationship occurs with the textual relationship, in the very next chapter. There, Skúli is introduced as the brother of Heimir, foster-father of Brynhildr in *Völsunga saga* and guardian of her daughter Áslaug, Ragnarr's second wife, in *Ragnars saga*—indeed, the narrator stresses that this is the same Heimir *er getr í sögu Ragnars konungs loðbrókar* 'who is mentioned in the saga of King Ragnarr loðbrók' (Guðni Jónsson 1954, IV 249). This textual reference to *Ragnars saga* is one of four explicit references that the beginning of *Hálfdanar saga* makes to other texts or narrative traditions, the others being to Eiríkr víðförli (from *Eiríks saga víðförla*), Hrómundr Gripsson (from *Griplur/Hrómundar rímur Gripssonar* and *Hrómundar saga Gripssonar*) and *Landnámabók*. It seems clear, therefore, that *Hálfdanar saga* uses *Ragnars saga* for solely decorative purposes. If we also examine the differences in the two sagas' manifestations of ATU 510A's structure—most notably, though not limited to, *Ragnars saga*'s lack of a garment as proof of identity—it seems clear that although the two sagas have an explicit connection in some aspects, they are entirely independent of each other as Cinderella variants.

The full extent of ATU 510A's influence on *Hálfdanar saga* is somewhat shrouded by the fact that several aspects common to many variants of the tale type have obviously been superseded in the saga by tropes which are standard to *fornaldarsaga* narratives. For instance, while the source or instigator of aid in ATU 510A variants is often a maternal figure of some kind, Skúli is male—but his custodianship of Princess Ingigerðr after the death of her parents nonetheless makes him a substitute parental figure, and his concealment of the princess mirrors the narrative function of the female Silven in *Vilmundar saga*. The parental figure's gender and status in *Hálfdanar saga* were probably the natural result of the saga author's construction of a geopolitical landscape typical of the *fornaldarsögur*, namely one which was male-dominated and whose power hierarchies revolved around the king. Similarly, Hálfdan's primary motivation behind his search for Ingigerðr is not to find his prospective bride, as might be expected of an ATU 510A variant, but rather to avenge his father. Vengeance for a murdered family member is a recurring theme in the legendary sagas, but in *Hálfdanar saga* this motivation never comes to fruition, and, in fact, its chief outcome is to bring Hálfdan back into contact with his prospective bride. It seems, therefore, that the core ATU 510A structure is deeply embedded in the saga, even if many familiar aspects of variants of the tale type were overlaid by standard *fornaldarsaga* elements. This process of literary construction can be somewhat illuminated by comparing certain elements with their parallels in the closely related *Vilmundar saga*, and perhaps the most significant element of all is the manifestation of the identifying garment.

The presence of the garment alone seems to suggest that *Hálfdanar saga* is a product of a different Cinderella tradition from that of *Eskja* and *Ragnars saga*. However, despite its close parallels with *Vilmundar saga*, there are two significant differences between the two sagas' manifestations of the motif. The recognition process is very close in both sagas, namely, the missing garment being produced, and, along with the princess's ring and hand, serving to verify her identity to the hero. However, the initial loss of the garment is a point of difference: only in *Vilmundar saga* does the hero find and keep the shoe. In *Hálfdanar saga*, Hálfdan has the tables turned on him when the disguised Ingigerðr recovers her glove and ring and flees, cursing him to be without peace until both are freely given to him. Cinderella figures do not usually recover the lost garment as soon as they lose it, but in *Hálfdanar saga* the heroine does so—probably because the saga author considered this to be the most realistic way to have Hálfdan later recognise Ingigerðr without her male disguise—and the theme of losing the garment, which usually affects the heroine/princess, has instead been transferred to the hero, Hálfdan. This has the effect of delaying the imbuing of the garment with marital associations; it is only when Ingigerðr later gives Hálfdan the glove that it becomes a marriage pledge. This delay is necessary in the narrative context because Hálfdan's chief motivation—and therefore the driving force of the latter half of his saga—is vengeance for his murdered father, and not a bridal quest.

The slipper test has been central to symbolic readings of ATU 510A, such as Bruno Bettelheim's psychoanalytical analysis of the tale, in which he argues that the slipper is a symbolic representation of the vagina, and that Cinderella's act of placing her foot into the shoe signifies her own acceptance of a marital and sexual relationship with the prince (Bettelheim 1976, 270–71). *Hálfdanar saga* must be briefly discussed in this light, because the sequence of events within Hálfdan's first meeting with Ingigerðr may seem symbolically distinct from most ATU 510A variants, in that the eventual groom prematurely removes the garment from the eventual bride, only to have her take it back almost immediately. However, as with other aspects of the saga described above, this turn of events seems to have been constructed simply to treat Ingigerðr's disguise more logically from a *fornaldarsaga* point of view: Ingigerðr was disguised as a man when she first met Hálfdan; so in order for him to recognise her at their second meeting without her disguise, it would make narrative sense for her to have retained the garment to prove her identity. Furthermore, the saga author probably did not intend any symbolism in having Hálfdan rather thoughtlessly take the glove as opposed to having Ingigerðr accidentally leave it; the authorial motivation behind this turn of events seems to have been to enable the use of the *álög* 'curse' motif. This motif, which involves the laying of a curse or taboo with highly specific effects and conditions for release, is very common in Icelandic romances, and was ultimately derived from the Irish *geis* (see Einar Ólafur Sveinsson 1957, 19–20, and Power 1987). Finally, perhaps the strongest indication that the first meeting between Hálfdan and Ingigerðr was not designed with much symbolism in mind is the fact that the glove is treated perfunctorily when they eventually meet again.

The second major difference in the treatment of the 'slipper' test motif in *Hálfdanar saga* and *Vilmundar saga* is the garment itself: it is a glove in the former, and a shoe in the latter.[36] The shoe is an ancient allomotif, as it is found in the early Cinderella tales of Rhodopis and Ye Xian, whose earliest literary attestations come from the first century BC and ninth century AD respectively. Indeed, *Vilmundar saga*'s version of the motif as a whole is far closer to those earlier Cinderella tales than it is to *Hálfdanar saga*: Sóley loses her shoe and states it to be a token of marriage before it is found by Vilmundur, who later returns it and marries her. We have also seen an indication that *Vilmundar saga* was influenced by a source in which the shoe had a 'perfect fit' function, which is hinted at in *Vilmundar saga* but never developed.[37] We can therefore assume that the shoe was the original object in the source that influenced *Hálfdanar saga* and *Vilmundar saga*. This would suggest the following: that *Hálfdanar saga* and *Vilmundar saga* were both influenced by a Cinderella tale; that

---

[36] In the *Motif-Index*, H114, 'Identification by glove', is in fact listed as a motif separate from the slipper test (H36.1). The sole example provided of H114 is the Middle English romance *Sir Degaré*, in which a glove, with which the hero had been abandoned as an infant, serves to prove the hero's identity to his mother, just in time to prevent them from consummating their incestuous marriage.

[37] In neither *Vilmundar saga* nor *Hálfdanar saga* is the garment a 'perfect fit' for the princess in a physical sense—it is sufficient for her to be the owner of the item, and she is never specified to be the only person on whom the garment will fit, nor does she need to undergo a test to prove that it does belong to her.

Hálfdanar saga modified the slipper test motif to suit its narrative demands; and that *Vilmundar saga*, despite borrowing the character assemblage of *Hálfdanar saga*, chose to retain the original form of the motif. This suggests that a Cinderella tale containing the shoe must have been known in Iceland by the fourteenth century. However, there is little else that we can definitively say about this hypothetical source tale, other than that it could well have been oral.

The possible influence of *Þiðreks saga* on the use of the shoe motif in *Vilmundar saga* must be briefly noted. We have already seen in Section 2 that *Þiðreks saga* had a relatively minor textual influence on *Vilmundar saga*; it is interesting that it should also contain a bridal shoe of a sort. It is found in the story of King Ósantrix of Vilkinaland. In seeking the hand of Princess Oda of Húnaland, Ósantrix has sent several messengers to the Hunnish court, all of whom have been thrown into prison (though Oda herself has received the suit favourably). Taking matters into his own hands, the disguised Ósantrix enters the hostile Hunnish court with his men, intending to infiltrate it. However, the Hunnish king Milias wisely chooses to dismiss him, prompting Ósantrix's men to launch an immediate and successful attack on the court. Oda is then brought before the victorious Ósantrix, without knowing who he is. Ósantrix first places a silver shoe on her foot, which fits perfectly, before he replaces it with a golden shoe, which is stated to be even more fitting for her than the silver shoe, presumably because of its higher value. Oda then declares her wish to be near King Ósantrix, and he reveals himself to her. Not long afterwards, they are married.

It is quite clear that this episode, which *Þiðreks saga* borrowed directly from the twelfth-century Middle High German poem *König Rother* (Cox 1892, xl–xli; Andersson 1974, 5), is substantially different from the accounts of the bridal garments in *Vilmundar saga* and *Hálfdanar saga Eysteinssonar*. First, there are two shoes. Second, *Þiðreks saga* lacks the theme of loss: the shoes are never possessed by Oda in the first place, who therefore cannot lose them for her eventual husband to find. Third, both shoes are overtly emphasised to be a perfect fit on Oda's foot, an aspect missing from *Hálfdanar saga* and *Vilmundar saga*. The functions of loss and perfect fit were distinct features of the Cinderella tale as far back as Rhodopis, so the discrepancies are significant. The motif in *Þiðreks saga* (and *König Rother*) was apparently derived from an old German betrothal custom, in which 'the bridegroom brings it [the shoe] to the bride, and as soon as he has placed it on her foot she is regarded as subject to his authority' (Cox 1892, 505). Any possible influence that the Ósantrix

Introduction xliii

episode in *Þiðreks saga* could have had on the shoe motif in *Vilmundar saga* was probably limited to the shoe's ceremonial function as a symbol of marriage, as well as its prestigious gilding. In other words, *Vilmundar saga* could not have derived the iconic and ancient motif of the princess' lost shoe from *Þiðreks saga*, but the prestige of Sóley's shoe is at least one parallel to the Ósantrix-Oda episode. Unfortunately, owing to the incalculability of oral sources, it is difficult to read any significance into this thinnest of connections.

2e.iv. *The Cinder-name*

While *Vilmundar saga* is the earliest extant source for the shoe motif in Scandinavia, it has a significance even more remarkable and global than this. Folklorists have long assumed that it was with Basile's seventeenth-century Cenerentola that literary Cinderella variants began to contain cinder-names; that is, the name relating to the heroine's work in the hearth. However, *Vilmundar saga* also contains a cinder-name: *Öskubuska*, with *ösku-* deriving from *aska* 'ashes'. This name is still the modern Icelandic name for Cinderella today, although its literary origin in *Vilmundar saga* is unknown even to many Icelanders. *Vilmundar saga* is thus the earliest known Cinderella variant in the world to contain a cinder-name, by at least two centuries.

The main question to be addressed, therefore, is where the name *Ösku-buska* came from. Indeed, how this name came to exist in *Vilmundar saga* is an important question for the study of the transmission of ATU 510A, not least because the heroine's overt association with the hearth, and the cinder- or ash-name deriving from it, is a key element of 'Cinderella' in the modern public consciousness. Indeed, this element, whose first manifestation in a literary Cinderella story was long thought to be Basile's tale, has become an essential part of many Cinderella variants written (or recorded) after the seventeenth century, by virtue of becoming a defining aspect of the heroine's identity. Thus we find a variety of different hearth-names, sometimes even within the same country. Apart from *Cenerentola* and *Cendrillon*, examples of such names from Cox's collection of variants include the Danish *Askepot* (Cox no. 42) and *Askenbasken* (no. 62); Norwegian *Aaskepot* (no. 80); Swedish *Askungen* (no. 22) and *Aske-Pjeske* (no. 115); German *Aschenputtel* (no. 37), *Aschengrittel* (no. 74), and *Aschenbrödel* (nos 19, 53 and 56); Istrian *Conçaçienara* (no. 52); Russian *Chernushka* (no. 16) and Scottish *Ashpitel* (no. 4). Yet this specific association with the hearth was not a core part of Cinderella tales before the seventeenth century, and this is reflected in the fact that no variant predating the seventeenth century contains a hearth-name—with the curious exception of *Vilmundar saga*.

In her seminal work on the Cinderella cycle, Anna Birgitta Rooth (1980, 110) pointed out that the development of hearth-names in Cinderella stories was an exclusively European feature, arguing that they 'entered the tradition in the Balkan area' (111). Her argument was based on two premises. First, she pointed out that 'hearth-cat' nicknames are prevalent in Balkan and southern European sources (Rooth 1980, 111–12, especially 112 n. 1), with one such source being Basile's relatively early version from the seventeenth century. Second, she suggested that the Greek Cinderella name, Σταχτοπούττα (*Stachtopoutta*), seemingly first appearing in print in 1832 (Cox no. 17), might be rendered 'hearth-cat', and that the latter element (πούττος [*pouttos*], the female reproductive organs, on which a cat might sit in the σταχτή [*stachte*] 'ashes') was the ultimate origin of forms like the German *Aschenputtel*, Danish *Askepot* and Scottish *Aessiepattle*.[38] She bases this argument on the fact that 'only in the Greek the name seems to possess any real meaning but in other tongues it appears to be cases of a popular etymological adaptation of a foreign word to conform with a common one' (Rooth 1980, 112). In other words, it seems that Rooth did not see any shared significance in the possible derivation of *-puttel* from Low German *pudeln* or Central German *puddeln* (both meaning 'to dig', cf. modern German *buddeln*), or *-pattle* from Middle English *padell* (referring to a spade-like tool, cf. modern English *paddle*), but instead considered such elements to have been chosen because of their phonetic similarity to the Greek word, to the extent that some cases are even apparently nonsensical as stand-alone elements, such as the Danish *-pot*.

Rooth's speculative argument, however, can only apply to Cinderella-names which share a similar-sounding latter component (such as *-puttel*, *-pot*, *-pattle*), or to Cinderella-names from stories demonstrably influenced by this Balkan/southern European tradition of hearth-cat names (and which would therefore probably be younger than the earliest literary attestation of that tradition, Basile's 'Cenerentola'). Öskubuska of *Vilmundar saga* is neither. The first element of her name is the standard hearth-related element, *ösku-* deriving from *aska* 'ashes', and this will be discussed later. The second element, however, is slightly more ambiguous. The word *buska* does not appear in any dictionaries of Old Norse, and seems only to have been attested as a stand-alone Icelandic word

---

[38] Rooth derived the interpretation of the Greek term, along with its possible feline association, from Philip Argenti and H. J. Rose (1949, I 443, n. 1).

from the seventeenth century onwards (Ásgeir Blöndal Magnússon 1989, 94), meaning that we cannot be absolutely certain what it meant in the fourteenth or fifteenth centuries, or whether *Vilmundar saga* influenced the definitions of this word. Nonetheless, Ásgeir Blöndal Magnússon suggests two feasible definitions, both connected with a sixteenth-century noun, *buski*. First, *buska* could refer to a *lauslát flökkukona* 'promiscuous vagrant-woman', relating to the definition of the noun *buski* as a small forest (with cognates in modern English *bush*, German *Busch* and Italian *bosco*).[39] However, *buska* could also be a verb for sweeping, and *buski* could also refer to a brush. Assuming either or both of these meanings were in currency by the fourteenth century, Öskubuska's name could therefore mean 'Ash-tramp' or 'Ash-sweep'. Öskubuska is initially a promiscuous kitchen servant but later becomes an exile in the forest—by curious chance, both meanings are highly applicable to her![40]

Partly because we cannot be entirely sure whether *buska* held either or both of the above meanings in the fourteenth century, the chicken-and-egg question over which of the two, Öskubuska's name or narrative function, influenced the other in the composition of *Vilmundar saga* is ultimately speculative. For instance, we cannot categorically rule out the possibility that *Vilmundar saga* derived the name from a separate, pre-existing Cinderella tale and simply adapted Öskubuska to live up to her name. Certainly the extent to which oral traditions lie behind the fantastic sagas of the fourteenth century cannot be overstated (Mitchell 1991, 46–47). However, there is a plausible literary process through which the name could have been coined (which may in turn have been influenced by a pre-existing Cinderella tale), and the solution lies in *Hálfdanar saga Eysteinssonar*. As stated in Section 2d, *Vilmundar saga* and *Hálfdanar saga* contain three pairs of parallel characters who fulfil similar functions early on, giving the sagas similar dramatic trajectories. The strong slave Kolr in *Hálfdanar saga* maps onto the strong slave Kolur in *Vilmundar saga*, and the runaway Russian princess Ingigerðr in *Hálfdanar saga* maps onto the runaway Russian princess Sóley in *Vilmundar saga*. Öskubuska's corresponding character in *Hálfdanar*

---

[39] Guðmundur Andrésson (1683, 22) suggested that *buska* could refer to the daughter of a convicted outlaw. This definition also implies a derogatory reference to the woman's social class and status as an outsider.

[40] Because Öskubuska's character so closely matches the distinctly specific definition of 'promiscuous vagrant-woman', it is tempting to think that this was the meaning the saga author intended.

saga is the serving-girl Ingigerðr (Kolsdóttir). This Ingigerðr is, conveniently enough, both namesake and *doppelgänger* of Princess Ingigerðr of Aldeigjuborg, and the two switch appearances to help the princess avoid an unwanted marriage in the face of imminent invasion. This is in fact Ingigerðr Kolsdóttir's most important narrative function, as she does little of significance throughout the rest of the saga and is eventually said to have drowned (Guðni Jónsson 1954, IV 277)—an ignominious end for an insignificant character.

In comparison, Öskubuska plays an expanded role in *Vilmundar saga* as a minor but actively antagonistic character after her initial function of supporting the princess. Having already been established as Kolur's sexual partner early in the saga, her fierce fight with Vilmundur later elevates her to the role of Kolur's partner-in-crime (more specifically, his partner in robbery, physical strength and monstrosity). The fact that her strength rivals even that of Vilmundur makes her one of the saga's most formidable antagonists, despite the paucity of her appearances. Because Öskubuska represents such an expansion on the corresponding figure of *Hálfdanar saga*'s Ingigerðr, it is unsurprising that she should have her own name, instead of sharing a name with the princess.

This in itself does not explain why Öskubuska should have a hearth-name, but it does point us in a helpful direction, namely the special relationship between Öskubuska and Kolur kryppa. This relationship begins not long after Kolur is put to work in the king's household, and the monstrous fighting prowess that they both develop later in the saga proves theirs to be something of a match made in hell. The couple are so perfect a fit that they are reminiscent of the Jungian archetype of the *syzygy* (which denotes the twinning of a pair of basic opposites such as masculinity and femininity; Jung 1968, 65), and this suggests that Kolur and Öskubuska were specifically designed as counterparts to each other, rather like a twisted Adam and Eve. For Öskubuska this process is particularly emphasised because, unlike Kolur, she has a different name from her *Hálfdanar saga* counterpart. This coupling of Kolur and Öskubuska is significant on a semantic level because the name Kolur (meaning 'coal'),[41] is a hearth-name like *Öskubuska*. It is a common name in Old Norse literature, but in the case of *Vilmundar saga*, it was probably borrowed

---

[41] Deriving from *kolr* 'coal' is the compound noun *kolbítr* 'coal-biter', which refers to the common trope of a 'male-Cinderella figure, who appears to be lazy or slow-witted, but eventually proves himself' (Driscoll 2005, 200). The term implies that the *kolbítr*'s laziness involved lounging by the hearth.

directly from the corresponding figure of Kolr (Ingigerðr's father) in *Hálfdanar saga*. If we accept that Kolur and Öskubuska were consciously shaped as a matching couple, this suggests that Öskubuska could have been given a hearth-name specifically to match Kolur's. This in turn raises the possibility that Öskubuska's name and associated hearthside occupation came about, at least in part, as a creative expansion on the character arrangement of *Hálfdanar saga*, although it should be stressed that this does not preclude the incalculable possibility of influence from a separate, concurrent oral tradition containing a hearthside character with a hearth-name.

There is one final observation to make about the cinder-name in the context of *Vilmundar saga*. It has been suggested above that the cinder-name and the shoe motif—neither of which exists in *Eskja*—could quite feasibly have entered *Vilmundar saga* through different pathways, one a creative decision in the composition of the saga, the other a remnant of a pre-existing source. This separation between the two elements is borne out on a basic narrative level. The incorporation of the hearth-name may be a product of the Kolur-Öskubuska relationship, but the shoe motif centres on the Sóley-Vilmundur narrative arc and has nothing to do with either Kolur or Öskubuska. The shoe has no relevance before it is lost, and it is only lost after Sóley and Öskubuska have already switched appearances and parted, never to encounter each other again. In other words, the cinder-named character has nothing to do with the Cinderella shoe. This strongly reinforces the remarkable likelihood that the co-occurrence of the two elements in *Vilmundar saga*—and therefore the saga's status as the earliest known Cinderella tale with a cinder-name by some two centuries—is a complete and utterly fortuitous coincidence.

This analysis has shown that the unmistakeable Cinderella variant that is *Vilmundar saga* is at least partly the product of multiple routes of traceable literary transmission of the tale type. The texts discussed by no means make up the complete picture of the transmission of the Cinderella tale type in medieval Iceland; apart from other literary sources that may have been lost, nothing definitive can be said about any oral sources, which are very likely to have played a role in the transmission of key motifs. On the basis of the texts that do survive, though, the relationships between them can be seen in the diagram below (where a single arrow represents influence, a double arrow represents faithful translation, a line without arrowhead represents non-Cinderella-related influence and a dotted line represents a hypothesised influence of unknown date):

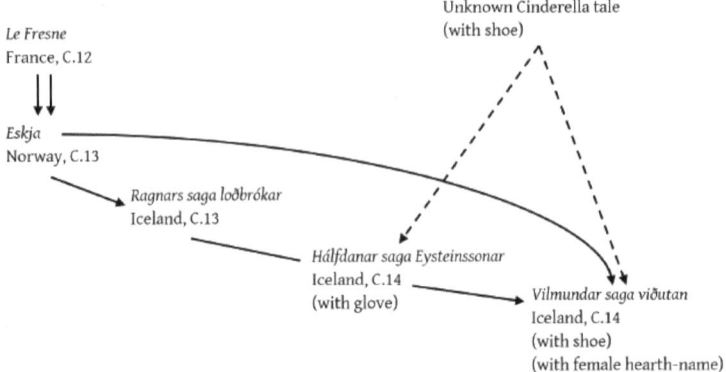

Eskja, the Norwegian translation of Marie de France's *Le Fresne*, is a crucial part of the picture. Not only is it a Cinderella variant itself, by virtue of being a faithful translation of *Le Fresne*, but it also had a major influence on both the trajectory of Áslaug's relationship with Ragnarr in *Ragnars saga* and the narrative circumstances of the persecuted heroine in *Vilmundar saga*—crucial aspects of the Cinderella structures of both. These aspects, therefore, can ultimately be traced back at least to twelfth-century France, via Norway.

Ragnars saga seems to have had no direct influence on *Vilmundar saga*, although, in an intriguing coincidence that has nothing to do with Cinderella, the two sagas do share an indirect connection, in that they happen to be the two narrative traditions to which *Bósa saga* sets itself up as a prequel. *Bósa saga*'s ending establishes the heroes Bósi and Herrauðr as the grandfather of Vilmundur viðutan and the father-in-law of Ragnarr loðbrók respectively (Guðni Jónsson 1954, III 321–22), but this coincidence, a product of the interconnection of literary traditions within the corpus of the medieval *fornaldarsögur*, has no bearing on the sagas' significance as Cinderella variants. This interconnection is also responsible for *Ragnars saga*'s superficial genealogical link with *Hálfdanar saga Eysteinssonar*, which has nothing to do with the Cinderella elements in either.

Not only is *Hálfdanar saga* the most significant literary influence on *Vilmundar saga*, but it also constitutes, with *Vilmundar saga*, a branch of the Cinderella folktale tradition independent of that of *Eskja* and *Ragnars saga*, namely one containing a bridal garment. The fact that *Vilmundar saga* deploys a shoe rather than a glove, despite the overwhelming influence of *Hálfdanar saga*, suggests that the ancient allomotif of the shoe was probably part of this branch of the Cinderella folktale. The differences between the two sagas' Persecution and Aid episodes prove that *Vilmundar saga* represents a fusion of at least two separate Cinderella narrative traditions which were circulating concurrently in fourteenth-century Iceland.

Although *Ragnars saga loðbrókar*, *Hálfdanar saga Eysteinssonar* and *Vilmundar saga viðutan* are sagas of medieval composition, their individual narrative traditions continued to thrive long after the Middle Ages. Each saga would continue to be copied in manuscripts in Iceland until the early twentieth century, and their stories were also converted multiple times into verse ballads in Iceland and the Faroe Islands in the post-medieval period. One curious point to note is that there is an Icelandic folktale, the 'Tale of Mjaðveig', first recorded in the nineteenth century, which came to be referred to in scholarship as 'the Icelandic story of Cinderella' (Carpenter 1880, 237–49; Carpenter summarises two variants of the same tale). This tale has some noticeable parallels with contemporary Cinderella variants from abroad, but bears virtually no resemblance to any of the medieval Icelandic Cinderella variants discussed here, which is all the more intriguing given that the three sagas were still being actively copied into manuscripts at a time when the Mjaðveig tale was in oral circulation. This is a reminder of the inevitable plurality in folktale transmission, a reality already demonstrated in the very individuality of the texts and traditions discussed. From *Eskja* to *Vilmundar saga*, from the ash-tree to the ashes-tramp, the Cinderella tale took on a different form with each new literary iteration. Indeed, each iteration crystallised, often in understated fashion, the branch of the Cinderella tradition to which it belonged, but in the rare and remarkable case of *Vilmundar saga* two branches became fused in a single text, resulting in a saga which is not only the earliest known Cinderella variant from Scandinavia to contain the iconic shoe, but also the earliest known Cinderella variant in the world containing an ash-name. More locally, *Vilmundar saga* can lay claim to a place of significance in modern Icelandic culture: Öskubuska is still the Icelandic name for Cinderella today.

3. Manuscripts and Editions

As stated above, *Vilmundar saga* survives in some form in fifty-four known manuscripts. The *Bibliography of Old Norse-Icelandic Romances* lists forty-nine of them (Kalinke and Mitchell 1985, 130–31), while the *Stories for All Time* website lists three manuscripts containing excerpts or summaries of the saga: AM 576 c 4to (1690–1710); NKS 1144 fol. (first half of the eighteenth century); and NKS 1685 b 4to Part II (first half of the nineteenth century). There are also two other known manuscripts which contain the saga but are not listed in Kalinke and Mitchell's bibliography: Lbs 4920 8vo and Lbs 5170 8vo (which is a fragment of the middle part of the saga).[42] Only three of these manuscripts, AM 586 4to, AM 343 a 4to and AM 577 4to, are medieval. Because we have so few surviving manuscripts, it is difficult to speculate on the popularity of *Vilmundar saga* in the late medieval period. However, the fact that Vilmundur is named in *Allra kappa kvæði* suggests that by this point he was at least as well-known as the many other heroes of fantastic sagas alongside whom he is named—despite the fact that the line concerning Vilmundur only says *Vilmund utan vél gékk flest* 'most things went well for Vilmundur *utan* (from the outside)' (Cederschiöld 1883, 64, st. 7). Further evidence for Vilmundur's popularity in the sixteenth century can be seen in the production of two sets of *rímur*. One set of *Vilmundar rímur* was written by a certain 'Ormur', formerly identified by scholars as Ormur Loftsson; but this is unlikely to be correct given that this Ormur died in 1446 (Foote 1962, 11–12). The other was written by Hallur Magnússon (d. 1601). While Hallur Magnússon's *rímur* formed the basis of a younger prose version of *Vilmundar saga* (surviving in three manuscripts, JS 411 8vo, ÍBR 49 4to and Lbs 1445 8vo),[43] only Ormur's *Vilmundar rímur* have been edited (Ólafur Halldórsson 1975).

Three post-medieval sets of *rímur* were also produced, written by a farmer called Guðni Jónsson in 1815 (not to be confused with the editor of the popular 1954–59 edition of *fornaldarsögur*); Hafliði Finnbogason in 1860; and Jón Sigurðsson in 1884 (Finnur Sigmundsson 1966, 501–03). None of these post-medieval *rímur* have been edited. Taking into account also the large number of eighteenth- and nineteenth-century manuscripts of *Vilmundar saga*, it is clear that the popularity of the Vilmundur tradition continued to thrive, even while younger romance sagas were being created, popularised and written into manuscripts during these centuries.

---

[42] The 'Lbs' shelfmark denotes a manuscript from the collection of the Landsbókasafn Íslands (National Library of Iceland). Many thanks to Sigríður Hjördís Jörundsdóttir of the Manuscript Department for making the author aware of these two manuscripts.

[43] A manuscript from this younger prose tradition in turn spawned a nineteenth-century Faroese ballad, *Vilmunds kvæði* (Glauser 1993, 702), listed in the *Corpus Carminum Faeroensium* as no. 104. The 'JS' and 'ÍB' shelfmarks denote manuscripts from the collections of Jón Sigurðsson and the Icelandic Literary Society in Copenhagen respectively. Both collections are now held in the National Library of Iceland.

The three medieval manuscripts containing *Vilmundar saga* are AM 586 4to, AM 577 4to, and AM 343 a 4to. All three are quite typical of compilations of *fornaldarsögur* and *riddarasögur*: they are anonymous, low-grade, lacking in images or decoration, cramped for space, and, in their current state, defective in some places. Of the three medieval manuscripts, the text in 586 is the fullest, and has been used as the base text of the critical editions of both Nils William Olsson (1949) and Agnete Loth (1964), as well as the present edition. 586, which is dated to 1450–99, comprises thirty-three folios, and it contains six fables followed by eight sagas (some in defective form), *Vilmundar saga* being preceded by *Bósa saga* and followed by *Hálfdanar saga Eysteinssonar*. Although they have been discussed earlier, the strong relationships that *Vilmundar saga* has with these sagas cannot be overstated; with *Bósa saga* in particular, the *Vilmundar saga* of 586 shares literary parallels, genealogical connection, adjacent positions in the manuscript, and scribal hands. The manuscript also contains several other romance sagas, including a defective version of *Hrings saga ok Tryggva*, another borderline *fornaldarsaga* based in Garðaríki. *Hrings saga* follows *Hálfdanar saga* in the manuscript, meaning that, along with *Vilmundar saga,* there are three consecutive legendary romances set in Garðaríki.

The name given by Árni Magnússon to 586 was Arnarbælisbók, presumably because he acquired it from Arnarbæli in southern Iceland (Loth 1977, 23).[44] The same two scribes of 586 also produced AM 589 4to, previously a single codicological unit (or two) which has now been divided into six parts, consisting mostly of romance sagas (Loth 1977, 7).[45] Árni received the six parts of 589 from Björn Þorleifsson, who was born in Oddi and educated at Skálholt (both in southern Iceland). Björn would become bishop of Hólar in northern Iceland, but only after he had given 589 to Árni (Loth 1977, 23). Wherever they were produced, these two manuscripts, written by the same scribes and both containing a number of adventure romances, were acquired separately from southern Iceland.

---

[44] Agnete Loth (1977, 23) notes that 'three other manuscripts in the Arnamagnæan Collection come from Arnarbæli, AM 135 4to, AM 160 4to and AM 573 4to'; the former two are law-books, and the last contains *Breta sögur* and *Trójumanna saga*.

[45] The various parts of 589 contain *Kirjalax saga, Samsons saga fagra, Valdimars saga, Klári saga, Ectors saga, Stúfs þáttr, Þorsteins þáttr bæjarmagns, Egils saga einhenda, Hálfdanar saga Brönufóstra, Álaflekks saga, Hákonar saga Hárekssonar, Sturlaugs saga starfsama* and *Göngu-Hrólfs saga* (Loth 1977, 7–8).

By contrast, 343a is known to be of northern origin, having been written at the farm of Möðruvellir fram (Orning 2015, 59–65). Produced in 1450–75, it is roughly contemporaneous with 586, and its text of *Vilmundar saga* is close to that of 586, not only textually, but also in terms of phonology. In these two manuscripts—but not in 577—'the [linguistic] trend in the direction of modern Icelandic . . . is still in the developmental stage' (Olsson 1949, xi). Accordingly, it has been argued that they are 'based on the same prototype' (Olsson 1949, xi; Schröder 1917, 76). The textual evidence supports a strong relationship between the two, most notably in their agreement over two key elements which differ in 577: Kolur's nickname, *kryppa*; and the provocative ending—although in 343a, we cannot be sure that the second half of this was indeed the exhortation to 'kiss Öskubuska on the arse', because it has been scraped from the manuscript and written over.

343a is a much larger manuscript than 586, containing fifteen sagas and one fable in its 110 folios. It has been mentioned in Section 2d that geographic unity may have been an important factor in the manuscript's compilation. It contains five legendary sagas with a significant Russian setting, three sagas involving the semi-mythical kingdom of Glæsisvellir, and all four Hrafnista sagas (the only extant medieval manuscript to do so). *Vilmundar saga* fits in the manuscript as a whole on both generic and geographical grounds, but, as in 586, its position in the manuscript may be telling: it follows two fragments of *Bósa saga*, which follows *Hálfdanar saga Eysteinssonar*. On the balance of literary evidence, there is a real likelihood that *Vilmundar saga* was deliberately placed near these two sagas in both 586 and 343a—two out of three of its extant medieval manuscripts—which would indicate that literary connections were a defining factor in the saga's early transmission.

Vilmundar saga's third medieval witness, 577, also dates from the second half of the fifteenth century, but may have been written slightly later than 586 and 343a (Olsson 1949, xi). In its eighty-two surviving folios, it contains six legendary romances and a fable, and all but one text (*Vilhjálms saga sjóðs*) are now defective.[46] The 577 text of *Vilmundar saga* is very consistent with that of 586 and 343a in terms of narrative substance, and largely consistent in terms of vocabulary and phrasing, but it contains a critical difference: the cognomen of the troublesome thrall Kolur is not *kryppa* 'hunch' but *kroppinbakur* 'hunchback'. The nouns

---

[46] Apart from *Bósa saga*, the only other saga to travel in 586, 343a and 577 is *Flóres saga konungs ok sona hans*, a romance. In that saga, as in *Vilmundar saga*, we also find a foster-mother character named Silven.

kroppur and *kryppa* are semantically interchangeable,[47] but because cognomens form a concrete part of character identity, the variation here is significant, not least because there is an identically named character in another *fornaldarsaga*, *Þorsteins saga Víkingssonar*.[48] Together with smaller pieces of evidence such as minor syntactical variation, this indicates that the text of 577 belongs to a separate stemmatic branch from that of 586 and 343a, and that this divergence of separate branches happened early in the history of the saga, that is, by the time the three manuscripts were written in the second half of the fifteenth century. The orthography of the 577 text also differs from that of 586 and 343a, in that it exhibits more younger features which reflect the phonological changes that had taken place over the fourteenth and fifteenth centuries (Olsson 1949, xi).

All three medieval manuscripts were taken to Copenhagen as part of Árni Magnússon's ambitious manuscript collecting around the turn of the eighteenth century.[49] Most of the surviving witnesses of the saga were written in Iceland after this undertaking, and they could therefore not have been copied directly from 586, 343a or 577. Yet we can be sure that a close witness or witnesses of the saga remained in Iceland after 586, 343a and 577 were taken. We can adduce this through the general uniformity of the tradition of post-medieval witnesses. Most of these seem to be based on the branch of the *Vilmundar saga* tradition to which 577 belongs. With one exception, all post-medieval witnesses which are not copies of 586 give Kolur's cognomen as *kroppinbakur*,[50] and they also follow 577 in

---

[47] For instance, *Partalopa saga*, a *riddarasaga*, introduces the monstrous figure of Gramur with a *kroppur* in one manuscript and a *kryppa* in another (Præstgaard Andersen 1983, 98).

[48] In *Þorsteins saga Víkingssonar*, the character named Kolr kroppinbakr is the sorcerous King of Indíaland. He plays the smallest of roles in that saga, being mentioned only as the father of a number of monstrous children (Guðni Jónsson 1954, III 3–8), but as the word *kroppinbakur* only seems to appear here and in *Vilmundar saga*, it is highly probable that the character from *Þorsteins saga Víkingssonar* had an influence, whether direct or indirect, on the variant cognomen found in 577. On a tangential note, a version of *Sturlaugs saga starfsama* contains a similarly named character, Kolr krappi.

[49] All three manuscripts have since been returned to Iceland. 343a was transferred to the Stofnun Árna Magnússonar in 1976, 586 in 1978 and 577 in 1987.

[50] JS 411 8vo, written in Iceland sometime in the eighteenth or nineteenth centuries and one of three manuscripts (along with Lbs 1445 8vo and ÍBR 49 4to) containing the younger redaction of the saga based on Hallur Magnússon's *rímur*, gives Kolur's cognomen as *krippabakur*.

omitting to mention Sviði's cognomen (*hinn sókndjarfi* 'the Battle-Bold') and his relationship to Bósi. Furthermore, none of them contain the R-rated ending of 586.

The fact that these post-medieval witnesses are virtually all from the 577 branch rather than the 586/343a branch indicates that the 577 branch was probably the only version of the medieval saga available to later scribes. It seems that few or no manuscripts of the 586/343a branch of the saga survived to be copied in Iceland after 586 and 343a themselves were taken to Denmark. By contrast, some manuscripts from the 577 branch must have remained in Iceland even after 577 had been taken to Denmark. These hypothetical intermediaries, which must have been produced sometime before the turn of the eighteenth century (possibly even during the medieval period) and then been copiously copied, are no longer extant. Yet the consistency of the post-medieval evidence that does survive would suggest that these hypothetical intermediaries were themselves reasonably consistent, and the tradition reasonably stable.

Although the text of *Vilmundar saga* remained very consistent overall throughout its transmission, its ending would undergo a late and very interesting development in several post-medieval witnesses. As in the 577 text, the majority of the saga's post-medieval witnesses simply end with Vilmundur and Hjarrandi settling down to rule their kingdoms, followed by a simple statement closing the saga (and lacking the provocatively humorous invocation of Öskubuska's posterior). However, a small number of witnesses from the eighteenth and nineteenth centuries end the saga with a brief mention of the children of Hjarrandi and/or Vilmundur.[51] The ending of Guðmundur Hjartarson's 1878 edition of the saga follows one (lost or unidentified) witness stemming from this tradition, appearing as follows (Guðmundur Hjartarson 1878, 35):

> Segja það aðrar sögur, að synir Hjaranda konungs hafi verið þeir Hárekr, Hrómundr, Herrauðr og Högni, er börðust við Andra jarl; enn Vilmundr hafi átt þann son, er nefndist Hernit inn frækni. Lúkum vér svo sögunni af Vilmundi viðutan.

> Other sagas say that the sons of King Hjarandi[52] were Hárekr, Hrómundr, Herrauðr and Högni, who fought against Jarl Andri; and Vilmundr had a son called Hernit inn frækni 'the Valiant'. Thus we end the saga of Vilmundr viðutan.

---

[51] At least four such manuscripts survive: ÍB 185 8vo (1760–80); JS 623 4to (1853–99); Lbs 4656 4to (1855–1860); and Lbs 1497 4to (1883).

[52] In almost all post-medieval manuscripts, the name of Hjarrandi in *Vilmundar saga* is spelled as *Hjarandi*.

Not all witnesses containing this genealogical ending give Hjarrandi as many as four sons (or Vilmundur even one), and there is striking variation among the few manuscripts that do provide a genealogical ending. For instance, the text in Lbs 1497 4to (written in 1883, not long after the publication of Guðmundur's *Sagan af Vilmundi viðutan*) lists Hjarandi's four children, but remarks of Vilmundur and Sóley that *ekki áttu þau barn saman svo ritað finnist* 'they did not have children together who are found to be written about'; while Lbs 2477 4to, which is dated to 1870–73, does not list any of Hjarandi's descendants, but names Vilmundur's son as Herrauður. In the addition of the particular genealogical ending in Guðmundur Hjartarson's edition, we may see a relatively young development in the Vilmundur tradition: the fusion with the tradition of *Andra saga jarls*. *Andra saga* is a reconstructed *fornaldarsaga* based on a set of fifteenth-century *rímur* (Jorgensen 1990, 188), which, in turn, seems to have been based on a lost medieval *Andra saga jarls (Mitchell 1991, 185).[53] In that tradition (saga and *rímur*) there exists a jarl named Hjarandi with four sons named as above, as well as a warrior named Hernit, but they appear unconnected to the Hjarrandi and Vilmundur of *Vilmundar saga*. For instance, that Hjarandi is given no backstory other than his status as a jarl of Elfey, a fictional location (Kuhn 2014, 26), while Hernit's parentage is never mentioned. Because *Andra saga* does not substantiate the connection between the Vilmundur and Andri traditions, it is apparent that the connection is superficial, hinging solely on the conflation of Prince Hjarrandi and Jarl Hjarandi. Nonetheless, this is an important development in the process of transmission of *Vilmundar saga*. It shows that although the saga was faithfully copied by all scribes, this did not preclude creative accretion. The creation of new genealogical associations and the fusion of heroic traditions shows that the saga was by no means a sacred medieval monument to be left untouched, but a living tradition to be adapted. This same impulse certainly underlies the composition of individual sets of *rímur* based on the saga, and possibly even the medieval insertion of the provocative ending into the 586 text.

On a tangential note, it is fascinating to note that the Vilmundur tradition was itself used as the object of the same sort of genealogical grafting by at least one other tradition: that of *Jasonar saga bjarta*, a little-known post-medieval romance that has never been published, and which only recently received its first substantial scholarly discussion (Wawn 2018).

---

[53] *Andra saga jarls* has only been published once, in 1895 as a popular edition, under the title *Saga af Andra jarli, Helga hinum prúða og Högna Hjarandasyni*.

In manuscripts of the longer version of *Jasonar saga*, the disguised Duke Herrauður reveals his true heritage to the saga's protagonist, Jason bjarti, declaring himself to be the grandson of Vilmundur viðutan. This moment is described as follows in *Jasonar saga*'s earliest extant manuscript, the eighteenth-century Lund, Universitets Bibliotek, MS 4 4to, as transcribed and translated by Andrew Wawn (2018, 244):[54]

> Nu skaltu vita ad heite mitt er Herraud*ur*. Er eg son*ar*son Vilmund*ur* vidutan*n* er v*ar* mikill hreiste mad*ur*.
>
> 'Now you shall know that my name is Herrauður. I am the grandson of Vilmundur the Outsider, who was a man of great valour.'

No extant manuscript contains both *Vilmundar saga* and a form of the Jason bjarti story (Wawn 2018, 245), but the fact that Vilmundur's tradition continued over time to build connections beyond its own narrative is further evidence for its popularity in eighteenth-century Iceland. Indeed, as both the subject and object of creative accretion in the form of various genealogical connections established across the centuries, from the late medieval to the post-medieval period, Vilmundur's tradition seems to have held an enduring status as a vibrant member of the literary ecosystem of Iceland.

The first printed edition of *Vilmundar saga* was published by Guðmundur Hjartarson in 1878, even as the saga continued to be copied in manuscripts. Guðmundur's was a popular rather than a critical edition, fully based on younger Icelandic manuscripts. Guðmundur notes in his afterword that the main manuscript on which his edition was based was written in the middle of the eighteenth century (1878, 36), and that he consulted other manuscripts as well. He also mentions that there were many manuscripts to which he did not have access; these would have included 586, 343a and 577, of which he was probably unaware, because they remained in Copenhagen until almost exactly a century after his edition was published. As stated above, the late genealogical addition to the end of *Vilmundar saga* is found in Guðmundur's edition, although it is difficult to identify the specific manuscript from which he derived it, because no known witness corresponds exactly to his ending.

No other edition of *Vilmundar saga* was produced until 1949, when Nils William Olsson edited it as part of his doctoral thesis. Although unpublished, this is nonetheless the only full critical edition of the

---

[54] I am grateful to Professor Wawn for directing me to several more manuscripts of the longer version of *Jasonar saga* in which the Vilmundur connection is present.

saga.⁵⁵ It was therefore the first edition for which the lacunae in the medieval manuscripts was a problem. None of the three medieval witnesses preserves the text in its entirety. The following diagram shows the lacunae in each of the three manuscripts; black areas represent sections of the text which are missing (chapter numbers correspond to the chapter numbers used in this volume):

As the diagram shows, 586 is by far the most complete extant manuscript of *Vilmundar saga*, with only a single lacuna beginning near the end of chapter 8, just after Silven's ironic remark that the 'princess' would be a suitable match for Kolur, and ending in chapter 11 with Vilmundur introducing himself to King Vísivalldur. The text in 577 has two lacunae before ending partway through chapter 12, with the description of Ruddi's nails. The first lacuna begins in chapter 3, with the description of Gullbrá's suitors requiring Hjarrandi's permission to speak with her; and the text begins again in chapter 5, just as Sóley is about to summon Öskubuska. The second lacuna begins halfway through chapter 9, midway through the description of Vilmundur's appearance as he leaves home; and the text begins again halfway through chapter 10, with Princess Gullbrá remarking that Vilmundur must be unused to social company. 343a lacks the saga's opening, with the text beginning just after chapter 11, just as Vilmundur encounters 'Öskubuska' in the kitchen. There is another lengthy lacuna, beginning halfway through chapter 13, immediately before King Vísivalldur's misguided release of the polar bear, with the text resuming at the introduction of Guðifreyr at the beginning of chapter 20.

Olsson used 586 as his base text, and filled its lacuna with 577 and then, in the small section between chapters 9 and 11 where both manuscripts have overlapping lacunae, from NKS 1250 fol.. This latter manuscript, as mentioned above, was copied from 586 between 1771 and 1779, by Markús Magnússon (1748–1825) in Copenhagen (Loth 1977, 14), and it appears that Markús filled the lacuna by copying the paper supplements of unknown provenance that had been inserted into 586 (Olsson 1949, x).

---

⁵⁵ Olsson's introduction and edition focus heavily on the medieval manuscripts, not least because he was unable to consult the 'approximately 25' post-medieval paper manuscripts in Iceland that he was aware of, owing to a lack of photostat and microfilm availability in Iceland at the time (Olsson 1949, v).

Olsson's editorial decisions would also form the basis of the third edition of *Vilmundar saga*, which was published in 1951 in the sixth volume of Bjarni Vilhjálmsson's six-volume *Riddarasögur* edition. Bjarni's edition is simply Olsson's text, normalised to modern Icelandic orthography (Bjarni Vilhjálmsson 1951, VI vii–viii), and, as a popular edition, it contains only the briefest of introductions and no critical notes.

The most recent edition of *Vilmundar saga* was produced by Agnete Loth, in the fourth volume of her five-volume *Late Medieval Icelandic Romances*. Published in 1964, Loth's edition is semi-diplomatic, with selected variant readings, and an English summary at the bottom of each page. Like Olsson, Loth based her text on 586 and filled the lacuna with the text of 577 where possible. Where she differs from Olsson is in filling the section of the lacuna where both 586 and 577 are defective; instead of NKS 1250 fol., she supplies a text from an earlier manuscript, GKS 1006 fol., which is dated to the seventeenth century and also seems to share a close relationship with 586 (for instance, it gives Kolur's cognomen as *kryppa*).[56]

The text of the present edition is based on the same base text (586) and the same two supplements (577 and GKS 1006 fol.) as those used in Loth's edition. The text, therefore, is extremely close to her edition, albeit in normalised orthography. Furthermore, for the latter half of the saga's epilogue, which is no longer visible to the naked eye, this edition has relied on Loth's reading. As part of the normalisation process, Loth's corrections have also been followed in the cases where the manuscript has minor errors in spelling (such as *Balluina* instead of *Ballduina* in line 37 of f.23v; Loth 1964, 88). The text presented here also has several minor differences from Loth's edition. Loth's less necessary emendations, where she uses the late-seventeenth-century manuscript AM 549 4to to change certain minor readings for readability (such as emending *En þa* 'and then' or 'but then', in AM 586 4to to *enda*, either 'indeed' or an elliptical and untranslated word, in AM 549 4to; Loth 1964, 184, 187), have not been followed. Furthermore, grammatical emendations have also been made from the manuscripts where Loth's edition, being semi-diplomatic, retained them; these emendations mostly concern verb forms, which were not always followed to the letter in scribal spelling. Two examples would be *mege þer* 'you may' (Loth 1964, 173; the form used in this text is *megið þér*) and *munu uær* 'we will' (Loth 1964, 187; the form used here is *munum vér*). Similarly, on the rare occasions that numerals appear in the

---

[56] The case for the relationship between the texts of 586 and GKS 1006 fol. is slightly hampered by the fact that the latter is missing the ending of the saga.

manuscript, they have been written out here (such as *tólf* 'twelve', instead of the manuscript's *xii*, at the end of chapter 1). Punctuation, capitalisation of proper nouns, and paragraph divisions have all been supplied as part of the normalisation here; they are not present in the manuscripts used. The chapter divisions, however, are present in the manuscripts.

In his recent edition of *Illuga saga Gríðarfóstra*, for which his base text was from the mid-seventeenth century, Philip Lavender chose to regularise to seventeenth-century Icelandic rather than standard Old Norse, arguing that 'it would be misleading to normalise the text to Old Norse, a standard based on common philological and orthographical features of the thirteenth and fourteenth centuries' (Lavender 2015a, xxx). Following this rationale, the orthography of this edition of *Vilmundar saga* is a version of standardised Old Norse that has been normalised to reflect the linguistic changes that the Icelandic language had undergone by the fifteenth century. The reason for this is that the base manuscript is from the late fifteenth century, and thus the text is (mostly) a fifteenth-century version of *Vilmundar saga*. The normalisation adopted here differs from standardised Old Norse in the following aspects:

– Inclusion of the svarabhakti vowel (also known as u-epenthesis), e.g. *Vilmundur* instead of *Vilmundr*

– Fricativisation of *-k* in unstressed word-final position, e.g. *mjög* instead of *mjök*

– Fricativisation of *-t* in unstressed word-final position, e.g. *mikið* instead of *mikit*

– Diphthongisation preceding *-ng* and *-nk*, e.g. *Eingland* instead of *England*

– Diphthongisation of *-vá* to *-vo*, e.g. *svo* instead of *svá*

– Dental *l* preceding *-t* and *-d* represented as *-llt* and *-lld*, e.g. *Vísivalldur* instead of *Vísivaldur*

– Merging of *-rl* and *-ll* clusters, e.g. *kall* instead of *karl*

– Middle voice inflections ending in *-zt* instead of *-sk* or *-st*, e.g. *settizt* instead of *settisk* or *settist* (the *-zt* ending is also a distinct orthographical feature of 586)

All of these changes appear in the text of the base manuscript, albeit with some degree of variation in consistency. For instance, the svarabhakti vowel and the fricativisation of *-t* only appear infrequently, but even this is sufficient evidence that the linguistic changes represented by this orthography were under way. There are also cases of the scribes overcompensating in their attempts to use archaic forms; for instance, the plural noun *sögur* 'stories' on f.19r appears without the *-u* that is in fact part of its inflection and not the svarabhakti vowel. Rather more consistent are the diphthongisations and the *-zt* middle voice inflections. To the student learning standard Old Norse, the orthography of the text in this volume will undoubtedly seem unfamiliar, but with the help of the above list of normalised features, as well as the parallel translation, it is hoped that this inconvenience will not be too great a hindrance in enjoying this entertaining and important saga.

Finally, several words of thanks must go to a number of people and organisations without whose help this volume could not have been produced: to Sigríður Hjördís Jörundsdóttir and the team at the Handritadeild Landsbókasafn Íslands for granting the author access to all of their thirty-three post-medieval manuscripts containing the saga, as well as dealing so promptly and helpfully with other requests such as manuscript digitisation; to Haukur Þorgeirsson at the Stofnun Árna Magnússonar for providing scans of AM 343 a 4to that are not yet available online; to Rose Williamson Guy (University of Chichester) for helping me find my feet in the world of folklore and of Cinderella; to Matthew Driscoll and Philip Lavender (both of the University of Copenhagen) for kindly looking over and commenting on the draft manuscript; and most of all to Védís Ragnheiðardóttir (University of Iceland) and Brynja Þorgeirsdóttir (University of Cambridge) for their comprehensive suggestions at various stages of the translation process.

Bibliography

Aðalheiður Guðmundsdóttir 2009. 'Af Ingigerði Ólafsdóttur'. In *38 vöplur bakaðar og bornar fram Guðrúnu Ingólfsdóttur fimmtugri 1. maí 2009*. Ed. Guðvarður Már Gunnlaugsson, Margrét Eggertsdóttir and Þórunn Sigurðardóttir, 7–9. Reykjavik: Menningar- og minningarsjóður Mette Magnussen.

Aðalheiður Guðmundsdóttir 2014. '*Strengleikar* in Iceland'. In *Rittersagas: Übersetzung, Überlieferung, Transmission*. Ed. Jürg Glauser and Susanne Kramarz-Bein, 119–32. Tübingen: A. Francke Verlag.

Anderson, Graham 2000. *Fairytale in the Ancient World*. London: Routledge.

Andersson, Theodore M. 1994. 'Composition and Literary Culture in *Þiðreks saga*'. In *Studien zum Altgermanischen: Festschrift für Heinrich Beck*. Ed. Heiko Uecker, 1–23. Berlin and New York: de Gruyter.

Argenti, Philip Pandely and H. J. Rose 1949. *The Folk-lore of Chios*. Cambridge: The University Press.

Bachman, William Bryant and Guðmundur Erlingsson, trans, 1993. *Six Old Icelandic Sagas*. Lanham, MD: University Press of America.

Bertelsen, Henrik, ed., 1905–11. *Þiðriks saga af Bern* I. Copenhagen: Møller.
Bettelheim, Bruno 1976. *The Uses of Enchantment: The Meaning and Importance of Fairy Tales*. New York: Alfred A. Knopf.
Bibire, Paul 1985. 'From riddarasaga to lygisaga: The Norse response to romance'. In *Les Sagas de chevaliers (Riddarasögur): Actes de la Ve Conférence Internationale sur les Sagas*. Ed. Régis Boyer, 55–74. Paris: Presses de l'Université de Paris-Sorbonne.
Bjarni Aðalbjarnarson, ed., 1945. *Heimskringla* II. Íslenzk fornrit XXVII. Reykjavik: Hið íslenzka fornritafélag.
Bjarni Vilhjálmsson, ed., 1954–59. *Riddarasögur* I–VI. Reykjavik: Íslendingasagnaútgáfan.
Bjarni Vilhjálmsson and Guðni Jónsson, eds, 1943–44. *Fornaldarsögur Norðurlanda* I–III. Reykjavik: Bókaútgáfan forni.
Blöndal, Sigfús 1920–24. *Íslensk-dönsk orðabók*. Reykjavik: Gutenberg.
Bornholdt, Claudia 2011. 'The Old Norse-Icelandic Transmission of Chrétien de Troyes' Romances: *Ívens saga*, *Erex saga*, *Parcevals saga* with *Valvens þáttr*'. In *The Arthur of the North: The Arthurian Legend in the Norse and Rus' Realms*. Ed. Marianne E. Kalinke, 98–122. Cardiff: University of Wales Press.
Bruckner, Matilda Tomaryn 2006. 'LeFresne's Model for Twinning in the Lais of Marie de France'. *Modern Language Notes* 121, 946–60.
Carpenter, William H. 1880. 'The Icelandic Story of Cinderella'. *Folk-Lore Record* 3, 237–49.
Cook, Robert and Mattias Tveitane, eds and trans, 1979. *Strengleikar: An Old Norse Translation of Twenty-one Old French Lais*. Oslo: Norsk historisk kjeldeskrift-institutt.
Cox, Marian Roalfe 1893. *Cinderella: Three Hundred and Forty-Five Variants of Cinderella, Catskin, and Cap O' Rushes, Abstracted and Tabulated with a Discussion of Medieval Analogues and Notes*. London: David Nutt.
Cross, Samuel Hazzard 1929. 'Yaroslav the Wise in Norse Tradition'. *Speculum* 4, 177–97.
Djurhuus, N. and Chr. Matras, eds, 1944–46. *Føroya Kvæði: Corpus Carminum Faeroensium* [based on the work of S. Gruntvig and J. Bloch]. Copenhagen: Munksgaard.
Dresvina, Juliana 2009. 'St Cinderella, a Virgin Martyr: Literary and Iconographic Translations of the Legend of St Margaret of Antioch'. In *Lost in Translation?* Ed. Christiania Whitehead and Denis Renevey, 218–96. Turnhout: Brepols.
Dresvina, Juliana 2016. *A Maid with a Dragon: The Cult of St Margaret of Antioch in Medieval England*. Oxford: Oxford University Press.
Driscoll, Matthew James 2003. 'Fornaldarsögur Norðurlanda: The stories that wouldn't die'. In *Fornaldarsagornas struktur och ideologi*. Ed. Ármann Jakobsson, Annette Lassen and Agneta Ney, 257–67. Uppsala: Uppsala Universitet.
Driscoll, Matthew James 2005. 'Late Prose Fiction (*lygisögur*)'. In *A Companion to Old Norse-Icelandic Literature and Culture*. Ed. Rory McTurk, 190–204. Oxford: Blackwell.

Dundes, Alan, ed., 1988. *Cinderella: A Casebook*. Madison, WI: University of Wisconsin Press.
Einar Ólafur Sveinsson 1957. 'Celtic Elements in Icelandic Tradition'. *Béaloideas* 25, 3–24.
Einar Ólafur Sveinsson 2003. *The Folk-Stories of Iceland*. Ed. Anthony Faulkes, trans. Benedikt Benedikz. London: Viking Society for Northern Research.
Einar Sigurðsson 1962. 'Vilmundar saga viðutan'. Unpublished Master's thesis. University of Iceland.
Ellis Davidson, Hilda 1991. 'Gudmund of Glasisvellir: Did He Originate in Ireland?' *ARV: Scandinavian Yearbook of Folklore* 47, 167–78.
Finch, R. G., ed. and trans., 1965. *The Saga of the Volsungs*. London: Thomas Nelson and Sons.
Finnur Jónsson 1924. *Den oldnorske og oldislandske litteraturs historie* III. Copenhagen: G. E. C. Gads.
Finnur Jónsson and Eiríkur Jónsson, eds, 1892–96. *Hauksbók, udgiven efter de Arnamagnæanske håndskrifter no. 371, 544 og 675, 4°, samt forskellige papirshåndskrifter af det Kongelige nordiske oldskrift-selskab*. Copenhagen: Thiele.
Finnur Sigmundsson 1966. *Rímnatal* I. Reykjavik: Rímnafélagið.
Foote, Peter G., ed., 1962. *Lives of saints: perg.fol.nr.2 in the Royal Library, Stockholm*. Early Icelandic Manuscripts in Facsimile IV. Copenhagen: Rosenkilde and Bagger.
Glauser, Jürg 1983. *Isländische Märchensagas. Studien zur Prosaliteratur im spätmittelalterlichen Island*. Basel: Helbing and Lichtenhahn.
Glauser, Jürg 1993. '*Vilmundar saga viðutan*'. In *Medieval Scandinavia: An Encyclopedia*. Ed. Phillip Pulsiano and Kirsten Wolf, 702–03. New York and London: Garland.
Glauser, Jürg and Gert Kreutzer, trans, 1998. *Isländische Märchensagas* I. Darmstadt: Wissenschaftliche Buchgesellschaft.
Guðmundur Andrésson 1683. *Lexicon Islandicum sive Gothicæ runæ vel lingvæ septentrionalis dictionarium*. Havniæ [Copenhagen]: C. Weringii.
Guðmundur Hjartarson, ed., 1878. *Vilmundar saga viðutan*. Reykjavik.
Guðmundur Ólafsson, ed., 1694. S*agan af Sturlauge hinum Starf-sama eller Sturlög then Arbetsammes Historia. Fordom på gammal Göthiska skrifwen, och nu på Swenska uthålkad*. Uppsala.
Guðni Jónsson, ed., 1954. *Fornaldarsögur norðurlanda* I–IV. Akureyri: Íslendingasagnaútgáfan.
Hall, Alaric et al., eds and trans, 2010. '*Sigurðar saga fóts* (*The Saga of Sigurðr Foot*): A Translation'. *Mirator* 11, 56–91.
Hall, Alaric, Haukur Þorgeirsson and Steven D. P. Richardson, eds and trans, 2013. '*Sigrgarðs saga frækna*: A normalised text, translation, and introduction'. *Scandinavian-Canadian Studies* 21, 80–155.
Hughes, Shaun F. D. 2008. '*Klári saga* as an Indigenous Romance'. In *Romance and Love in Late Medieval and Early Modern Iceland: Essays in Honor of Marianne Kalinke*. Ed. Kirsten Wolf and Johanna Denzin, 135–64. Ithaca, NY: Cornell University Press.

Hui, Jonathan Y. H. 2018. 'Cinderella in Old Norse Literature'. *Folklore* 129:4, 353–74.
Hui, Jonathan Y. H., Caitlin Ellis, James McIntosh, Katherine M. Olley, William Norman and Kimberly Anderson 2018. '*Ála flekks saga*: An Introduction, Text and Translation'. *Leeds Studies in English* 49, 1–43.
Jiriczek, Otto Luitpold, ed., 1893. *Die Bósa-Saga in zwei Fassungen nebst Proben aus den Bósa-rímur*. Strassburg: Karl J. Trübner.
Jones, Steven Swann 1993. 'The Innocent Persecuted Heroine Genre: An Analysis of Its Structure and Themes'. *Western Folklore* 52, 13–41.
Jorgensen, Peter A. 1990. 'The Neglected Genre of Rímur-Derived Prose and Post-Reformation Jónatas saga'. *Gripla* 7, 187–201.
Jung, Carl G. 1968. *The Archetypes and the Collective Unconsciousness*. Trans. R. F. C. Hull. 2nd ed. Princeton, NJ: Princeton University Press.
Kalinke, Marianne E. 1985. 'Norse Romance (*Riddarasögur*)'. In *Old Norse-Icelandic Literature: A Critical Guide*. Ed. Carol J. Clover and John Lindow, 316–63. Ithaca, NY: Cornell University Press.
Kalinke, Marianne E. 1999. *Norse Romance II: The Knights of the Round Table*. Woodbridge: D. S. Brewer.
Kalinke, Marianne E. 2011. 'Arthurian Echoes in Indigenous Icelandic Sagas'. In *The Arthur of the North: The Arthurian Legend in the Norse and Rus' Realms*. Ed. Marianne E. Kalinke, 145–67. Cardiff: University of Wales Press.
Kalinke, Marianne E. and P. M. Mitchell 1985. *Bibliography of Old Norse-Icelandic Romances*. Ithaca, NY: Cornell University Press.
Kålund, Kristian 1888–94. *Katalog over den arnamagnæanske Håndskriftsamling*. Copenhagen: Gyldendalske Boghandel.
Ker, W. P. 1908. *Epic and Romance: Essays on Medieval Literature*. 2nd ed. London: Macmillan.
Kristensen, Evald T. 1881. *Æventyr fra Jylland*. Jyske Folkeminder IV. Copenhagen: K. Schønberg.
Kuhn, Hans 1990–93. 'The *Rímur*-Poet and his Audience'. *Saga-Book* 23, 454–68.
Kuhn, Hans 2000. 'Von Prosa zu Versgesang: Vilmundur viðutan in Saga, Rímur und Kvæði'. In *Erzählen im mittelalterlichen Skandinavien*. Ed. Robert Nedoma, Hermann Reichert and Günter Zimmermann, 47–74. Vienna: Praesens.
Kuhn, Hans 2014. '*Andra saga* und *Andra rímur*'. In *Erzählen im mittelalterlichen Skandinavien* II. Ed. Robert Nedoma, 24–44. Vienna: Praesens.
Lagerholm, Åke, ed., 1927. *Drei Lygisǫgur*. Halle (Saale): Max Niemeyer.
Larrington, Carolyne 2015. *Brothers and Sisters in Medieval European Literature*. Woodbridge and Rochester: York Medieval Press.
Lavender, Philip 2014. '*Illuga saga Gríðarfóstra* in Sweden: Textual Transmission, History and Genre-Formation in the Seventeenth and Eighteenth Centuries'. *Arkiv för nordisk filologi* 129, 197–232.
Lavender, Philip, ed. and trans., 2015a. *Illuga saga Gríðarfóstra*. London: Viking Society for Northern Research.
Lavender, Philip 2015b. 'The Secret Prehistory of the *fornaldarsögur*'. *Journal of English and Germanic Philology* 114:4, 526–61.

Lavender, Philip, trans., 2016. '*Þjalar-Jóns saga*: A Translation and Introduction'. *Leeds Studies in English* 46, 73–113.
Lockley, Mary L. R. 1979. 'An Edition of Samsons saga fagra'. Unpublished doctoral thesis. University of Birmingham.
Loth, Agnete, ed., 1964. *Late Medieval Icelandic Romances* IV. Copenhagen: Munksgaard.
Loth, Agnete, ed., 1977. *Fornaldarsagas and late medieval romances: AM 586 4to and AM 589 a-f 4to*. Early Icelandic Manuscripts in Facsimile, XI. Copenhagen: Rosenkilde and Bagger.
Lozzi Gallo, Lorenzo 2004. 'Persistent Motifs of Cursing from Old Norse Literature in *Buslubœn*'. *Linguistica e Filologia* 18, 119–46.
Lönnroth, Lars 2002. 'Dreams in the Sagas'. *Scandinavian Studies* 74:4, 455–64.
McKinnell, John 2005. *Meeting the Other in Norse Myth and Legend*. Woodbridge: D. S. Brewer.
McTurk, Rory 1977. 'The relationship of *Ragnars saga loðbrókar* to *Þiðriks saga af Bern*'. In *Sjötíu ritgerðir helgaðar Jakobi Benediktssyni 20. júlí 1977*. Ed. Einar G. Pétursson and Jónas Kristjánsson, 568–85. Reykjavik: Stofnun Árna Magnússonar á Íslandi.
McTurk, Rory 1991. *Studies in Ragnars saga loðbrókar and its Major Scandinavian Analogues*. Oxford: Society for the Study of Mediæval Languages and Literature.
McTurk, Rory 1997. 'Marie de France, *Geirmundar þáttr heljarskinns*, and reader-response criticism'. In *Hugur: mélanges d'histoire, de littérature et de mythologie offerts à Régis Boyer pour son 65e anniversaire*. Ed. Claude Lecouteux and Olivier Gouchet, 193–209.
Meulengracht Sørensen, Preben 2000. 'Social institutions and belief systems of medieval Iceland (*c*. 870–1400) and their relations to literary production'. Trans. Margaret Clunies Ross. In *Old Icelandic Literature and Society*. Ed. Margaret Clunies Ross, 8–29. Cambridge: Cambridge University Press.
Mitchell, Stephen A. 1991. *Heroic Sagas and Ballads*. Ithaca, NY: Cornell University Press.
Mundt, Marina 1973. 'Observations on the influence of *Þiðriks saga* on Icelandic saga writing'. In *The First International Saga Conference Edinburgh 21—29 August 1971*. Ed. Peter Foote, Hermann Pálsson and Desmond Slay, 335–59. London: Viking Society for Northern Research.
Müller, Peter Erasmus 1817–20. *Sagabibliothek* I–III. Copenhagen: Schultz.
O'Connor, Ralph 2005. 'History or fiction? Truth-claims and defensive narrators in Icelandic romance-sagas'. *Mediaeval Scandinavia* 15, 101–69.
Ólafur Halldórsson, ed., 1975. *Vilmundar rímur viðutan*. Reykjavik: Stofnun Árna Magnússonar á Íslandi.
Ólafur Halldórsson, ed., 2006. *Óláfs saga Odds*. In *Færeyinga saga. Óláfs saga Odds*. Íslenzk fornrit XXV. Reykjavik: Hið íslenzka fornritafélag.
Olsson, Nils William 1949. 'Vilmundar saga viðutan'. Unpublished doctoral thesis. University of Chicago.
Orning, H. J. 2015. 'Legendary sagas as historical sources'. *Tabularia* 15, 57–73.

Páll Eggert Ólason 1947. *Handritasöfn Landsbókasafnsins. I. Aukabindi*. Reykjavik: Landsbókasafn Íslands.
Power, Rosemary 1987. 'Geasa and Álög: Magic Formulae and Perilous Quests in Gaelic and Norse'. *Scottish Studies* 28, 69–89.
Præstgaard Andersen, Lise, ed., 1983. *Partalopa saga*. Copenhagen: Reitzel.
Quinn, Judy, et al. 2006. 'Interrogating Genre in the *fornaldarsögur*: Round-Table Discussion'. *Viking and Medieval Scandinavia* 2, 276–96.
Radt, Stefan, ed. and trans., 2005. *Strabons Geographika*: Band 4. Buch XIV–XVII: *Text und Übersetzung*. Göttingen: Vandenhoeck and Ruprecht.
Rafn, Carl Christian, ed., 1829–30. *Fornaldar sögur Nordrlanda eptir gömlum Handritum*. Copenhagen.
Rooth, Anna Birgitta 1956. 'Tradition Areas in Eurasia'. *Arv. Nordic Yearbook of Folklore* 12, 95–113.
Rooth, Anna Birgitta 1980. *The Cinderella Cycle*. Reprint. Lund: C. W. K. Gleerup.
Saga af Andra jarli, Helga hinum prúða og Högna Hjarandasyni 1895. Reykjavik.
Schier, Kurt 1970. *Sagaliteratur*. Stuttgart: J. B. Metzlersche.
Schlauch, Margaret 1934. *Romance in Iceland*. Princeton, NJ: Princeton University Press.
Schröder, Franz Rolf, ed., 1917. *Hálfdanar saga Eysteinssonar*. Halle (Saale): Max Niemeyer.
Shafer, John Douglas 2009. 'Saga Accounts of Norse Far-Travellers'. Unpublished doctoral thesis. University of Durham.
Shippey, Thomas A. 1988. 'Breton Lais and Modern Fantasies'. In *Studies in Medieval English Romances: Some New Approaches*. Ed. Derek Brewer, 69–91. Woodbridge: D. S. Brewer.
Simek, Rudolf 1986. 'Elusive Elysia, or: Which Way to Glæsisvellir? On the Geography of the North in Icelandic Legendary Fiction'. In *Sagnaskemmtun: Studies in Honour of Hermann Pálsson on his 65th Birthday*. Ed. Rudolf Simek, Jónas Kristjánsson and Hans Bekker-Nielsen, 247–76. Vienna: Böhlau.
Smithers, G. V., ed., 1987. *Havelok*. Oxford: Clarendon Press.
Staines, David 1976. 'Havelok the Dane: A Thirteenth-Century Handbook for Princes'. *Speculum* 51, 602–23.
Stefán Karlsson 2004. *The Icelandic Language*. Trans. Rory McTurk. London: Viking Society for Northern Research.
Stories for All Time. <http://fasnl.ku.dk/>.
Sverrir Jakobsson 2006. 'On the Road to Paradise: "Austrvegr" in the Icelandic Imagination'. In *The Fantastic in Old Norse/Icelandic Literature—Sagas and the British Isles. Preprint papers of the 13th International Saga Conference, Durham and York, 6th–12th August, 2006*. Ed. John McKinnell, David Ashurst and Donata Kick, 935–43. Durham: Durham University, Centre for Medieval and Renaissance Studies.
Thompson, Claiborne W. 1978. 'The Runes in *Bósa saga ok Herrauðs*'. *Scandinavian Studies* 50, 50–56.
Thompson, Stith 1946. *The Folktale*. New York: The Dryden Press.

Thompson, Stith 1955–58. *Motif-Index of Folk-Literature: A Classification of Narrative Elements in Folktales, Ballads, Myths, Fables, Mediaeval Romances, Exempla, Fabliaux, Jest-Books, and Local Legends*. Rev. edn. Copenhagen: Rosenkilde and Bagger.

Tolkien, Christopher, ed. and trans. 1960. *The Saga of King Heidrek the Wise*. London: Thomas Nelson and Sons.

Tulinius, Torfi H. 2002. *The Matter of the North: The Rise of Literary Fiction in Thirteenth-Century Iceland*. Trans. Randi C. Eldevik. The Viking Collection XIII. Odense: Odense University Press.

Uther, Hans-Jörg 2004. *The Types of International Folktales: A Classification and Bibliography. Based on the system of Antti Aarne and Stith Thompson*. 3 vols. Helsinki: Suomalainen Tiedeakatemia.

Waley, Arthur 1947. 'The Chinese Cinderella Story'. *Folklore* 58, 226–38.

Wawn, Andrew 2018. 'Jason bjarti in rímur and saga'. In *The Legendary Legacy: Transmission and Reception of the Fornaldarsögur Norðurlanda*. Ed. Matthew Driscoll, Silvia Hufnagel, Philip Lavender and Beeke Stegmann, 235–96. The Viking Collection XXIV. Odense: University Press of Southern Denmark.

Wilson, Nigel G., ed. and trans., 1997. *Aelian: Historical Miscellany*. Loeb Classical Library CDLXXXVI. Cambridge, MA: Harvard University Press.

Zitzelsberger, Otto J., ed., 1969. *The Two Versions of Sturlaugs saga starfsama: a Decipherment, Edition, and Translation of a Fourteenth Century Icelandic Mythical-Heroic Saga*. Düsseldorf: Michael Triltsch.

Þorleifur Hauksson, ed., 2007. *Sverris saga*. Íslenzk fornrit XXX. Reykjavik: Hið íslenska bókmenntafélag.

VILMUNDAR SAGA VIÐUTAN

THE SAGA OF VILMUNDUR THE OUTSIDER

Vilmundar saga viðutan

1. Vísivalldur[1] hefir kongur nefndur verið. Hann réð fyrir Hólmgarðaríki.[2] Hann var kvongaður, og hafði feingið dóttur kongs af Ungaría,[3] og er hún eigi nefnd. Kongur hafði ungur tekið við föðurleifð sinni. Hann var vaskur og vel siðaður og af öllum mönnum vel vingaður. Hann átti son, áður en hann giptizt, við einni jallsdóttur. Hann hét Hjarrandi. Hann var fríður maður sýnum og sterkur að afli og svo vel búinn að íþróttum, að fáir menn komuzt til jafns við hann. Hann var skjótráður og skörunglyndur, vinfastur og svo snarr í öllum atburðum, hvort hann var í bardögum eður burtreiðum, að því var til jafnað sem hvirfilvindur kæmi að, þar sem hann geystizt að fram, og því var hann kallaður Hjarrandi hviða.[4] Hann lá jafnan í hernaði, en var með föður sínum á vetrum.

Vísivalldur kongur átti að fara í kongastefnu eitthvert sinn, og var von, að hann væri í burtu meir en tólf mánaði. Drottning var með barni, og mjög fram komið, þá kongur fór heiman. Í þann tíma voru margir vísindamenn í Garðaríki, og kona ein var þar, sú er mest var tignuð af vísindamönnum, og létu ríkar konur jafnan sækja hana að mæla jóðmælum yfir börnum sínum, því að það gékk jafnan eptir, sem hún sagði fyrir. Drottning lét svo gjöra og bauð henni og gjörði á mót henni sæmiliga veizlu, en á meðan vísindakonan var þar, tók drottning sótt, en völvan sat yfir henni. Hún fæddi tvö meybörn, og voru bæði mikil og fögur. Völvan tók við meyjunum, og leggur þær niður á eina blæju, er á voru markaðar allra handa sögur. Þar lét hún upp á bera bæði gull og dýrgripi, blóm og alldin jarðar. Meyjarnar höfðu hönd í því sem hjá þeim lá, og tók sú er fyrr kom til einn skarifífil og bar í munn sér. Önnur tók einn gullbaug, og rann hann upp á hennar fingur. Völvan bar þá börnin til drottningar og mællti mörgum heillavænligum orðum yfir þeim. Hún sagði drottningu, að sú, sem gullbauginn tók, mundi verða kynsælli, og mundi gipt ágætum kongssyni, 'því að gull merkir kongatign, en sú, sem alldinið tók, mun vera fésæl og ársæl, og mun gipt bóndasyni af berserkjakyni, því að jarðarávöxtur merkir almúgann, og mun sá maður mikill fyrir sér, því að ekki alldin er jafnramt eður beiskara en skarifífill.'

---

[1] The name *Vísivalldur*, deriving from the Slavic *Vsevolod*, also means 'wise ruler' in Old Norse. See Section 2d of the introduction.

[2] *Hólmgarðaríki*, or *Garðaríki*, refers to the Kievan Rus'. Its capital was Hólmgarður, modern-day Novgorod. See Section 3d of the introduction.

[3] In *riddarasögur*, Úngaría, often translated as 'Hungary', seems to refer to a fictional kingdom in the east. It is also named in *Elis saga ok Rósamundu*, *Ívens saga*, *Nikulás saga leikara*, *Samsons saga fagra*, *Sigrgarðs saga ok Valbrands* and *Þiðreks saga*.

1. There was a king called Vísivalldur.[1] He ruled over Hólmgarðaríki.[2] He was a married man—he had taken to wife the daughter of a king of Úngaría,[3] but she is not named. The king had come to his inheritance young. He was valiant and well-mannered and friends with all men. He had a son before he was married, with the daughter of an earl. He was called Hjarrandi. He was a man handsome in appearance and great in strength, and so well-endowed with physical skills that few men were equal to him. He was impetuous and noble and loyal to his friends, and so swift in all situations, whether he was in battle or tournaments, that whenever he rushed forth, it was as if a whirlwind had arrived—and for this reason he was called Hjarrandi hvíða [gale].[4] He was constantly involved in warfare, but stayed with his father in the winter.

One time, King Vísivalldur had to go to a meeting of kings, and it was expected that he would be away for more than twelve months. The queen was with child and was very far along when the king left home. Many wise people were in Garðaríki at that time, but there was one woman who was honoured most out of the wise people. Powerful women frequently had her brought to speak birth-prophecies over their children, because what she prophesised normally came to pass. The queen had this done, inviting her and preparing for her an honourable feast. While the wise woman was there, the queen went into labour, and the seeress sat over her. She gave birth to two girls, both large and fair. The seeress took the girls and laid them down on a coverlet, on which were drawn all sorts of stories. There she had both gold and treasures laid, as well as flowers and fruits of the earth. The maidens took that which lay beside them, and the first one took a dandelion and put it into her mouth. The other took a golden ring, and it slid onto her finger. The seeress carried the girls to the queen and said many words of good luck over them. She told the queen that the one who took the gold ring would become more blessed with great offspring and would be married to a great prince, 'because gold marks royal dignity. But the one who took the plant will be wealthy and fertile and marry a farmer's son of berserk stock, because the fruit of the earth signifies the common people, and that man will be mighty, because no plant is as pungent or as bitter as the dandelion.'

---

[4] Curiously, a character named *Hjarrandi hvíða* also appears in the late twelfth-century *Sverris saga* (Þorleifur Hauksson 2007, 60, 181), a saga detailing the life of Sverrir Sigurðarson who ruled Norway from 1177 until his death in 1202. This Hjarrandi is a follower of King Sverrir, but he is only named twice in the saga, and it is difficult to see any connection between him and his *Vilmundar saga* namesake.

Hún gaf nafn meyjunum, og skal sú heita Sóley, er alldinið tók, en hin Gullbrá, er gullið tók upp,[5] og þakkar drottning henni góð ummæli, og var hún með góðum gjöfum í burt leyzt. Litlu síðar tók drottning sótt og andaðizt, og þótti þat mikill skaði, og var hennar útferð sæmiliga gjört á þann hátt, sem þá var siður til.

Kongur kom heim úr kongastefnunni, þá hann hafði rekið sitt erindi, og hafði hann frétt allt, áður en hann kom heim. Voru honum þá sýndar dætur sínar, og leizt honum vel á þær, og sýndizt honum þó Gullbrá miklu fríðari, en Sóley var skartsamlig og sköruglig, og þótti honum sem vera mundi skapmikil og hyggilig í bragði. Kongur lét fá henni fóstur í borginni, og hét sú kona Silven. Hún var við alldur. Hún átti dóttur væna, en maður hennar var dauður, og voru þær mæðgur mjög einar fyrir sér, og óx hún jafnan þar upp, þar til sem þær voru svo gamlar, að marka mátti, hverja náttúru hvor þeirra mundi hafa, fyrir þau atvik, er þær máttu sjálfar af sér víkja. Gullbrá var blíð og hýr og þýð við alla, og unnu henni allir hugástum, og óx hún upp í kongs höll og lék á lófum hverjum manni. Sóley var nokkuð fálátari, áfangamikil og veitul af fé, og sparði ekki við vini sína, og villdi hún og hafa það af hverjum, sem hún kallaði. Kongur unni henni minna, en þó voru þær systur báðar vinsælar, og fór svo fram, þar til er þær voru tólf vetra gamlar.

2. Hjarrandi lá í hernaði fyrir vestan haf og var frægur maður og fór vel með hernaði sínum. Hann var sigursæll. Þess er getið eitt sinn, at hann herjaði um Írland og lagði undir sig mikið af því. Írakongur sat í Gunnvalldsborg.[6] Hún var þar fjölmennuzt og ríkuzt. Sat Hjarrandi nú um borgina, en kongur leyndizt úr henni eina nátt við fá menn. Um morguninn eptir braut Hjarrandi borgina og rænti fé miklu, og brenndi síðan borgina. Og er hún brann, kom maður út úr steikarahúsi einu. Hann var mikill vexti og ljótur mjög. Hárið var brunnið af honum og skóklæðin neðan að kné. Hann hafði kistil mikinn á herðunum og lútur í hálsinum. Hann var illa eygður, en verr tenntur. Þeir gáfu honum grið, og spurðu hann að nafni. Han kvaðzt Kolur kryppa heita og vera þræll í borginni.[7]

---

[5] *Sóley* and *Gullbrá* mean 'Buttercup' and 'Gold-brow' respectively. In modern Icelandic, *Gullbrá* is the name of the saxifrage flower and the fairytale character Goldilocks.

[6] It is unclear whether Gunnvaldsborg can be identified with a real city. A city of the same name appears in *Óláfs saga helga*, in Snorri Sturluson's early thirteenth-century Separate Saga and in *Heimskringla* (Bjarni Aðalbjarnarson 1945, 24), but scholars have tentatively placed that Gunnvaldsborg in Spain.

She gave the maidens names, and the one who took the plant was to be called Sóley, and the one who took the gold Gullbrá.[5] The queen thanks her for her kind words, and she departed with good gifts. Shortly afterwards the queen fell ill and died, and that was considered a great tragedy. She was given an honourable burial in the way that was then customary.

The king returned home from the meeting of kings when he had completed his errand, and he had heard about everything before he arrived home. His daughters were then shown to him, and he was well pleased with them. Gullbrá seemed to him the more beautiful, but Sóley was extravagant and high-spirited, and it seemed to him that she would be haughty and wise in countenance. The king had her fostered in the city by a woman named Silven. She was getting on in years. She had a beautiful daughter, but her husband was dead; mother and daughter were very much alone. Sóley grew up there until the princesses became old enough that their nature might be discerned according to the quirks that they displayed. Gullbrá was gentle and cheerful and friendly with all, and everyone loved her wholeheartedly. She grew up in the king's hall, pampered in everyone's hands. Sóley was more reserved, but generous and open-handed with wealth, and she wasn't sparing with her friends, though she wanted everyone to do as she bade. The king loved her less than her sister, but both sisters were still popular. Things went on like this until they were twelve years old.

2. Hjarrandi was engaged in warfare west of the sea. He was a famous man, and things went well with his battles—he was victorious. It is said that at one time he was pillaging in Ireland and subjugated much of it under himself. The Irish king was staying in Gunnvaldsborg.[6] It was the wealthiest and most populous city there. Hjarrandi laid siege to the city, but the king stole away from it one night with a few men. The next morning Hjarrandi breached the city and plundered much wealth, burning the city afterwards. And as it burned, a man came out of a kitchen. He was large in size and very ugly. His hair was burnt off, as well as his shoes beneath the knees. He had a large hump on his shoulders and he stooped at the neck. He had ugly eyes and worse teeth. The men gave him quarter and asked his name. He said that he was called Kolur kryppa [hunch] and was a thrall in the city.[7]

---

[7] As stated in Section 3 of the introduction, 577 and almost all post-medieval manuscript witnesses give Kolur's cognomen as *kroppinbakur*, but both 586 and 343a have *kryppa*.

Þessu næst fréttu þeir, að kongur safnaði liði, og varð landherinn svo mikill, að Hjarrandi hafði ekki við. Héllt hann þá burt af Einglandi, og austur aptur í Garðaríki.[8] Hann gaf föður sínum þrælinn, og setti kongur hann höfðingja yfir tólf þræla. Hann var svo mikill fyrir sér, að hann hafði vel tólf manna afl, til hvers sem hann gékk. Ambátt var sú ein þar í garðinum, er Öskubuska hét. Hún var stór vexti og sterk að afli, og var hún mjög fyrir öðrum ambáttum, og var vel með þeim Kol.

3. Hjarrandi hviða átti garð í borginni, og var hann sterkliga byggður. Héllt hann þar sína menn, en hann var í kongsgarði, en héllt þeim allan kost. Hjarrandi streingdi þess heit, að hann skal þeim einum manni gipta systur sína Gullbrá, sem jafn væri honum að öllum riddaraskap. Síðan lét hann gjöra kastala sterkan í borginni og færði þangað systur sína, og fékk til hertuga dætur og jalla að þjóna henni, og hæverskra sveina. Eingi maður skylldi svo djarfur vera, að geingi til tals við jungfrúna utan orlofs Hjarranda, en hver sem þess dirfizt, þá er hans höfuð af höggvið og bundið við garðstaur. En ef þeir menn kómu, sem biðja villdu jungfrúnnar, þá var þegar vís burtreið af hendi Hjarranda, og steypti hann öllum af baki, og misstu þeir bæði sæmd og fé. En ef þeir menn völlduzt til þess, sem honum þótti lítilræði við að eiga, þó að kyngóðir væri, þá lét hann höggva höfuð af þeim og festa við staur. En þá Hjarrandi var eigi heima, setti hann þann mann til að geyma turninn, er Ruddi hét. Hann var mikill og sterkur og illur viðreignar, og svo miskunnarlaus, að honum mátti ekki gott ætla. Fékk nú kongsgarðurinn kenningarnafn, og var kallaður Viðbjóður, því að flestir menn styggðuzt við að leggja þangað komur sínar.

Sóleyju var gjör skemma í borginni, og þjónuðu henni ríkra manna dætur, en allt var þar minna við haft en við Gullbrá, en Sóley var metnaðargjörn, og villdi ei hallda sig verr en systir hennar var halldin.

4. Maður er nefndur Úlfur hinn rammi, ríkur bóndi austarliga í Garðaríki. Hann var kallaður nokkuð grályndur og þó mikilmenni. Hann var kvongaður, og átti son, sá hét Úlfur illt eitt. Hann var hermaður mikill og óþýður, stirðlyndur og fégjarn og sjálfhælinn, og þó manna vaskaztur.

---

[8] The mention of England may be an error in 586. Apart from copies of that manuscript, all other manuscript witnesses, including 577, have *af Írlandi* 'from Ireland', which makes more sense in this context; and although it is certainly possible to sail from Ireland to Russia via England, nowhere else in the saga is England mentioned.

Next they learned that the king had assembled an army, and the ground force was so great that Hjarrandi could not match it. He then departed from England back eastwards to Garðaríki.[8] He gave the slave to his father, and the king placed him as chief over twelve thralls. He was so powerful that he easily had the strength of twelve men in whatever he did. There was a bondwoman in the household called Öskubuska. She was large in size and great in strength, and she was very much superior to the other bondwomen. She and Kolur got along well.

3. Hjarrandi hvíða owned a house in the city, and it was sturdily built. He accommodated his men there, and though he lived in the king's household, he covered all their expenses. Hjarrandi made the vow that he would only marry his sister Gullbrá to a man who was equal to him in all knightly accomplishments. Afterwards he had a strong castle built in the city and put his sister in it, charging the daughters of dukes and jarls as well as courteous squires to serve her. No man should be so audacious as to go to talk with the young lady without Hjarrandi's permission, and each person who dared had his head cut off and fixed on a stake. But if any men came forward who wished to ask for the young lady in marriage, then it was immediately certain that they had to joust against Hjarrandi, and he unhorsed them all, and they lost both honour and wealth. And if men whom he considered to be incompetent came forward for this, though they might be of good kin, he had their heads cut from them and fixed on a stake. When Hjarrandi was not at home, he appointed a man called Ruddi to guard the tower. He was big and strong, intractable and so merciless that one could not expect any good from him. The king's courtyard gained a nickname, and it was called Viðbjóður [Disgust], because most men avoided making their way there.

Sóley was built a small bower in the city, and she was attended by the daughters of powerful men, but she was attended less than Gullbrá in every way. But Sóley was ambitious and did not want to be held inferior to her sister.

4. There was a man called Úlfur hinn rammi [the Strong], and he was a wealthy farmer in the east of Garðaríki. He was said to be somewhat malicious, though a capable man. He was married and had a son called Úlfur illt-eitt [Only-Evil]. He was a great warrior, rough, cantankerous, greedy and boastful, though he was also the strongest of men.

Hann fór einn tíma til Hólmgarða með liði sínu þess erindis að biðja Sóleyjar. Silven fóstra hennar varð þess vör og sagði fóstru sinni. Sóley spyrr, hversu henni þætti þetta ráðligt. Hún kvað sér ekki á þetta lítazt, en kvað kong mundu gipta hana, hvað sem segði.

'Hvert traust skal ég þar eiga, sem þú ert?' segir Sóley.

'Máttur skal að megni þar um,' segir Silven.

Nú kemur Úlfur á kongs fund og hefir sitt mál frammi. Kongur fagnar honum vel og gjörði honum sæmiliga veizlu og sagði, að þeir skulu tala á morgun við hana, en segir það auðsott af sér, ef hún mællti ekki á móti. Fór Úlfur til tjalda sinna um kvölldið.

Þetta kvölldið kallar Sóley Kol kryppu til sín og mællti:

'Svo er háttað, Kolur,' kvað hún, 'að ég vil leggja trúnað undir þig. Hér er kominn Úlfur illt-eitt, son Úlfs hins ramma. Hann vill biðja mín, og er mér sagt, að kongur muni gipta mig, hvort ég vil eður eigi, en ég veit, að hann mun einskis ills svífazt, en ég vil eigi eiga hann, ef ég má öðru við koma. Því vil ég, að þú drepir hann fyrir mína skylld, og skalltu þá hafa fullkomna mína vináttu og kjósa þau laun, sem þú villt sjálfur kjósa.'

Kolur mællti: 'Því mun ég þat vinna,' segir hann, 'því að þá hefi ég kongs reiði og margra annarra góðra manna, og má ég þá kallazt drottinssvikari, og víst eigi einhlítur að komazt úr þessum vandræðum.'

'Allt vex þér í augu, örm mannskræfa,' segir hún, 'og má vera, að einnhver verði til annar, ef ég legg sjálfa mig í veð.'

'Eigi þarftu að frýja mér hugar,' segir Kolur, 'en ef þú villt sjálfa þig í veð setja, þá mun ég til voga, en óvíst þykki mér, hversu ég nýt þín, ef kongur verður var við.'

'Það mun eptir því, sem við verðum samráða,' kvað hún, 'og skalltu svo til haga, að þetta viti eingi utan við tvö, og skalltu þá gjöra kastala á skógi, og skulum við fara þangað, þegar uppvíst verður um okkur. Ég veit eigi, að mér muni annan bóndason betra að eiga en þig, ef það skal þó fyrir mér liggja.'

Og binda þau nú þetta fastmælum, og gefur hún honum eitt gull til trúskapar hér um.

5. Um náttina býr Kolur ferð sína til landtjallda Úlfs. Úlfur lét öngvan vörð hallda, og höfðu menn drukknir niður lagizt, og vissu sér einskis ótta von. Úlfur svaf í sæng, er Kolur gékk í tjalldið. Hann hafði mjótt járn í hendi og á tveir angar. Hann tekur upp skinnið undir hendi Úlfs, og stingur þar inn þessu járni, svo að stóð í hjartanu, en helldur saman skinninu

One time, he went to Hólmgarður [Novgorod] with his men for the purpose of asking for Sóley's hand in marriage. Her foster-mother Silven became aware of this and told her foster-daughter. Sóley asks how advisable that might seem to her. She said that she did not like it, but said that the king would marry her off regardless of what was said.

'How much support will I have from you?' says Sóley.

'Both might and main,' says Silven.

Then Úlfur comes to meet the king and puts forward his proposal. The king receives him well and prepared a splendid feast for him, saying that they would talk to her the next day, but he says that it would be fine by him, if she said nothing against it. Úlfur went to his tents in the evening.

That evening Sóley calls Kolur kryppa to her and said:

'It's come about, Kolur, that I want to put my trust in you. Úlfur illt-eitt, the son of Úlfur hinn rammi, has come here. He wishes to ask for my hand in marriage. I'm told that the king will give me to him whether I want it or not, but I know that he'll shrink from no evil, and I don't want to marry him if I can help it. Therefore I want you to kill him for my sake, and you'll then have my full friendship and can choose the rewards that you would like to have.'

Kolur said: 'Why would I do that, when I would then have the wrath of the king and many other noble men? I would be called a traitor to the king and it's not certain that I would get out of those troubles.'

'Everything looms large in your eyes, wretched coward,' she says, 'and it may be that someone else would be willing, if I offer myself as a pledge.'

'You don't need to challenge my courage,' says Kolur, 'but if you want to offer yourself as a pledge, I'll risk it, though it seems uncertain to me how I'll enjoy you if the king becomes aware of it.'

'It'll be as we agree upon,' she said, 'and you must arrange it so that no one will know of it except the two of us. You must then build a stronghold in the forest and we'll go there as soon as things about us are discovered. I don't think that any other farmer's son would be better for me to marry than you, if that's my fate.'

Now they bind fast their agreement, and to this end she gives him a gold ring as a pledge of fidelity.

5. During the night Kolur prepares for his journey to Úlfur's land tents. Úlfur had no one keeping watch, and the men had lain down drunk, not expecting any trouble. Úlfur was sleeping in his bed when Kolur walked into the tent. In his hand he had a slim piece of iron with two prongs. He slices open the skin under Úlfur's arm and thrusts the iron in so that it

fyrir utan, svo að allt blæðir inn,[9] og leggzt ofan yfir höfuðið á honum, svo að hann kom öngum hljóðum upp, og skillzt nú svo við hann, að hann myrðir hann sofanda, og urðu þeir eigi varir við, sem í tjalldinu voru.

Í þenna tíma hefir Sóley kallað til sín Öskubusku ambátt, og talar svo til hennar: 'Kaup vil ég við þig eiga,' segir hún.

'Hvern veg er því varið?' segir ambáttin.

'Ég vil, að við skiptum litum og klæðum,' segir Sóley, 'og skalltu fara í skemmu mína og nefnazt kongsdóttir og hátta svo öllu sem ég er vön. En ef Kolur kryppa kemur þar og heimtir nokkuð vilmæli að þér minna vegna, þá skalltu láta það allt satt vera, og gjör hans vilja í öllu, og alldrei skalltu láta hann annað vita, en þú sért kongsdóttir. En ég mun fara í steikarahús, og taka við þínum verknaði. Og hér til vil ég gefa þér minn gullhring.'

Öskubuska lét vel yfir þessu kaupi, og urðu þær kaupsáttar, og fór kongsdóttir í steikarahús, og var hún ill og öpr viðfangs, svo að eingi mátti við hana sæma. En Öskubuska fór í skemmu. Tóku meyjarnar við henni og þjónuðu henni vel, en hún var eigi vönd að. Matsveinum þótti hún taka vel til matar.

6. Um morguninn vakna menn Úlfs og finna hann dauðan, og leita nú og finna hvergi járnafar á honum, og kemur þeim það nú ásamt, að honum muni hafa verið gefið eitur að drekka, og var nú margrætt um þetta.

Koma nú þessi tíðindi fyrir kong, og líkaði honum það lítt, og mest af því að hann hugði, að aðrir mundu kenna honum um þetta. En með því að kongur var vinsæll, þá villdi eingi maður grun um það leiða, og fóru menn Úlfs nú heim, og var hann eigi mjög harmdauði, því hann var eigi vinsæll.

Nú er að segja frá Kol kryppu, að hann kom í skemmu kongsdóttur og heimti fram, það vilmæli er hún hafði lofað honum, en hún var í öngu bág, og lagði sig upp í hans valld, og létu þau það fara leyniliga og líða svo nokkurar stundir, og hafði Kolur nú sællífi mikið, og var eigi traust, að hann glettizt við skemmumeyjarnar,[10] og gjörði hann óléttar sex, kongsdóttir var og ólétt, og leyndi hver með annari.

[9] The phrase *blæða inn* also appears in *Sigurðar saga fóts*, another borderline *fornaldarsaga-riddarasaga*, and, as Alaric Hall et al. note in their edition of that saga, 'the idea seems to be that inward bleeding is mortally dangerous'. They also note the significant use of the phrase in *Njáls saga*, *Finnboga saga ramma*, *Finnboga rímur*, *Vilmundar rímur* and *Geðraunir*, the set of *rímur* on which the young prose version of *Hrings saga og Tryggva* was based (Hall et al. 2010, 84).

stood in the heart. Then he holds the skin together on the outside so that everything bleeds inwards,[9] and he lays himself down over Úlfur's head so that he could not make a sound. Then he parts with him, having murdered him in his sleep; and those who were in the tent were unaware of it.

In the meantime Sóley has called the bondwoman Öskubuska to her, and she speaks with her thus: 'I wish to make a deal with you.'

'In what way?' says the bondwoman.

'I want us to exchange appearances and clothes,' says Sóley, 'and you will go to my bower and call yourself the princess and act in every way as I am accustomed to. And if Kolur kryppa comes there and claims the fulfilment of a certain promise, you must act as if it is the whole truth and do his will in everything, and you must never let him suspect anything other than that you are the princess. But I will go to the kitchen and take over your work. To this end, I will give you my gold ring.'

Öskubuska was pleased with this arrangement, and they agreed the deal. The princess went to the kitchen, and she was ill-tempered and difficult to deal with, so that no one would put up with her. But Öskubuska went to the bower. The maidens attended her and served her well, and she was not fussy. The cooks thought that she took well to the food.

6. In the morning Úlfur's men awaken and find him dead. Then they search and find no iron-marks on him, and they agree that he must have been given poison to drink, and there was a great deal of discussion about that.

These tidings then come before the king, and he was displeased, mostly because he thought that others would implicate him. But because the king was popular, no one wished to lay suspicion on him for that, and Úlfur's men then went home. He was not greatly mourned because he was not popular.

Now it is to be told of Kolur kryppa that he came to the princess's bower and claimed what she had promised him, and she offered no objection and submitted herself to him, and they were secretive about that. Some time passes, and Kolur led a life of great enjoyment, and though it's by no means certain that he fooled around with the bower-maidens,[10] he made six of them pregnant, and the princess was also pregnant, although they hid it together.

---

[10] The phrase *var eigi traust* usually appears as a double negative (litotes), such as in *Þorsteins þáttr bæjarmagns* (ch. 13), *Þorsteins saga Víkingssonar* (ch. 23) and *Bárðar saga Snæfellsnáss* (ch. 1), with the sense 'it's not certain that he didn't…'. If a negative has been lost in *Vilmundar saga*, the loss occurred at an earlier stage of manuscript transmission than our earliest witnesses, since both medieval manuscripts containing this passage (586 and 577) have just the single negative.

7. Ásgautur hét jall; hann réð fyrir Aldeigjuborg.[11] Hann fór á fund Vísivallds kongs og bað Sóleyjar. Kongur tók því máli vel og sagðizt villdu tala þetta við dóttur sína. Nú sem kongsdóttir frétti þetta, segir hún frá Kol. Hann sagði, að þá mundi eigi setuefni, 'og munu við nú fara í þann kastala, sem ég hefi byggð, því við munum eigi geta dulizt leingur.' Kolur hafði gjört kastalann í stórum skógi, svo að luktuzt um hann hamrar, og mátti hann alldrei unninn verða. Ríður hann nú þangað og Sóley kongsdóttir með honum, að því sem hann hugði, og með þeim þeir tólf þrælar, sem í ráðum voru með Kol, og vantar þau nú ekki það, sem þau þurftu að hafa.

Um morguninn kemur kongur í skemmu dóttur sinnar, og var hún þá í burtu, og hefir hann nú sannar fréttir af því, að Kolur hefir drepið Úlf, en gjört óléttar allar meyjarnar, en tekið í burt dóttur hans, og líkar kongi nú allilla og þeim öðrum, sem feingið hafa skömm og skaða af þrælnum, og hér fyrir gjöra þeir Kol útlægan, og alla þá, sem honum fylgdu, og var gefið fé til höfuðs honum.

En er Kolur frétti sekt sína, hafðizt hann við á skóginum og hljóp opt í byggðina, og rænti fé miklu, en drápu menn, og gerðizt hann mjög óvinsæll. Hann blótaði eina gylltu, og varð hún svo mikil meinvættr, að hún drap bæði menn og fé, en spillti ökrum, bæði fyrir kongi og öðrum, og fór nú þessu fram leingi, og voru margar ferðir gerðar að Kol, og varð hann alldrei unninn, því að hann var bæði fjölkunnigur og mikill fyrir sér. Hjarrandi var nú þenna tíma í hernaði og sat stundum á vetrum í öðrum löndum.

8. Kall bjó í afdal langt í burt frá öðrum mönnum. Hann hét Sviði hinn sókndjarfi, son Bögu-Bósa.[12] Kelling hans hét Herborg.

Þau áttu son þann er Vilmundur er nefndur. Hann var mikill vexti, en sterkur að afli, og fríður sýnum, hærður manna bezt og eygður vel, skartsamligur á allan vöxt,[13] og voru þó menn andlitsfríðari, en þó villdu margir helldur hafa hans yfirlit, en hinna, er fríðari voru kallaðir.

Faðir hans hafði verið hinn mesti kappi, og því kenndi hann syni sínum íþróttir, sund og tafl og að skjóta og að skylmazt með skjölld og sverð, og var hann áskynja íþrótta, svo að faðir hans komzt um öngva til jafns við

---

[11] Aldeigjuborg is modern-day Staraya Ladoga, and is often translated as 'Ladoga Town'. It is a city in Garðaríki, and it plays an important role in *Hálfdanar saga Eysteinssonar*.

[12] As stated in Section 2c of the introduction, Bósi is one of the two eponymous heroes of *Bósa saga ok Herrauðs*. Sviði, his son, is named at the end of that saga, as well as in *Hálfdanar saga Eysteinssonar* and some manuscripts of *Illuga saga Gríðarfóstra*.

7. There was a jarl named Ásgautur, and he ruled over Aldeigjuborg [Ladoga Town].[11] He went to meet King Vísivalldur and asked for Sóley in marriage. The king took this proposal well and said that he would talk about it with his daughter. When the princess learned this, she tells Kolur about it. He said there would be no time to sit around, 'and now we will go to the stronghold that I have built, because we will no longer be able to remain hidden.'

Kolur had built the stronghold in a great forest so that it was encircled by cliffs. It could not be conquered. He rides there now with Princess Sóley (so he thought), and the twelve thralls who had been in Kolur's confidence were with them, and they have no lack of what they needed to have.

In the morning the king comes to the bower of his daughter, but she had disappeared, and he discovers the truth: that Kolur has killed Úlfur, impregnated all of the maidens and taken his daughter away. The king is scandalised, and so are the others who had suffered shame and damage at the hands of the slave. For this they have Kolur and all who followed him outlawed, and a price was put on his head.

When Kolur learned of his punishment he settled down in the forest and ran often to the village, looting plenty of livestock and killing men, and he became very unpopular. He sacrificed to a sow, which became such a monstrous being that it killed both men and livestock and despoiled cropland, that of both the king and others. That went on for a long time, and many forays were made to defeat Kolur, but he was never overcome, because he was both strong and skilled in sorcery. At the time Hjarrandi was engaged in warfare and sometimes spent winters in other lands.

8. There was a peasant who lived in a remote valley far away from other people. He was called Sviði hinn sókndjarfi [the Battle-Bold], son of Bögu-Bósi [Crippled-Bósi].[12] His wife was called Herborg.

They had a son named Vilmundur. He was large in size, mighty in strength and handsome in appearance, with fine eyes and the most exquisite hair of all men, extravagant in all proportions;[13] and although there were some men who were fairer of face, many would still rather have had his appearance than those of men who were called 'fair'.

His father had been a great champion, and so he taught his son his skills: swimming and chess, shooting and fencing with shield and sword. He became so proficient in these skills that even his father could not match

[13] The only characters in the saga to be called *skartsamlig(ur)* 'extravagant' are Sóley (in ch. 1) and Vilmundur, although in curiously different contexts.

hann. Móðir hans kenndi honum bóknæmi. Þá spyrr hann kall og kellingu, hvar menn allir voru, þeir sem sögur eru af gerðar. En þau sögðu honum, að menn voru þá allir dauðir, en tröll væri eptir í heiminum sumstaðar og dræpi þau menn, ef þau sæi þá, 'álfar lifa, og eru þeir í jörðu niðri.'
Kall átti margt ganganda fé, bæði geitur og hafra, yxn og gelldinga. Vilmundur geymdi jafnan að fénaði. Hann skaut opt dýr og fugla. Fór nú svo fram, þar til að hann var tvítugr að alldri.
Þat er nú sagt eitthvert sinn, að Vilmundur gékk um skóginn að leita geita sinna. Hann gékk þá upp úr dalnum, leingra en hann var vanur, og kom hann á sanda nokkura slétta. Þar var mörk breið öðrum megin. Hann gékk um sandinn, og var þar hlaðið saman steinum í nokkurum stað. Þar var í heitt vatn, svo að rauk af. Þá sá hann mannaspor, og hafði hann það eigi fyrr séð. Hann fann einn gullbúinn skó. Hann tók upp og geymdi. Hann sá einn stóran stein nokkuð svo frá lauginni. Þangað gékk hann til, því þangað lágu sporin. Hann gékk að steininum, og var gluggur á honum. Þar sá hann inni þrjár konur, og var ein við alldur, en tvær yngri. Þá mællti hin gamla kona:
'Hvað var nú tíðinda, fóstra mín, er þú fórt heiman?'
'Eingi voru tíðindi,' sagði hún, 'en það var þó nýjazt, að Kolur kryppa var gjör útlægur.'
'Hvað hafði hann til saka?' segir hin gamla kona.
'Eigi svo lítið,' segir hún; 'hann hafði blygðað allar skemmumeyjar, en gjört ólétta kongsdóttur.'
'Sú er honum maklig, kongsdóttirin,' segir hin gamla konan. Hún talaði þá til dóttur sinnar:
'Hvar eru skór fóstru minnar?' segir hún.[14]
En hún svipaðizt að og mællti síðan: 'Eigi hefir nú vel til tekizt. Hann hefir orðið eptir við laugina, en nú er svo framorðið, að þangað er ekki fært fyrir tröllagangi.'
'Slíkt er smáslys,'[15] sagði hin gamla kona, 'því at skór þessir voru dvergasmíði, og sú náttúra á, að þeir skylldu alldrei fyrnazt mega, en hún skylldi öngva skó aðra bera mega, og verður hún nú að ganga berfætt öðrum fæti.'

---

[14] According to the context, only one shoe is missing. By using the plural *eru* 'are', Silven is presumably asking a general question with an implied specific reference to the missing shoe.

[15] Loth emends *smáslys* 'small misfortune' to *stórslys* 'great misfortune', according to AM 549 4to, where the former reading was corrected to the latter at some point. However, the former reading, which is upheld in every other manuscript

him. His mother taught him book-learning. He asked his father and mother where all the people were who featured in stories. They told him that all the humans were dead, but that trolls still lived in some parts of the world, and that they killed humans if they saw them, 'and elves also exist, and they live down underground.'

The peasant owned much livestock, both billy and nanny goats, as well as oxen and wethers. Vilmundur frequently minded the livestock. He often shot beasts and birds. Things continued this way until he was twenty years old.

It it is now to be said that one time Vilmundur walked around in the forest to look for his goats. He walked through the valley and beyond, farther than he was used to, and he came to some sandy plains. There was a vast forest on one side. He walked around in the sand. In a certain place, there were stones that had been stacked together. Inside the stack was water so hot that steam rose from it. Then he saw human footprints, which he had never seen before. He found a gilded shoe, and he picked it up and kept it. He saw a large stone some way from the hot spring. He approached it, because the footsteps led towards it. He went up to the stone, and there was a window in it. He looked inside and saw three women there; one elderly and two younger. Then the old woman said:

'What tidings were there, my foster-daughter, when you left home?'

'There were no tidings,' she said, 'but this was the latest: that Kolur kryppa had been outlawed.'

'For what reason?' says the old woman.

'No mere trifle,' she says; 'he had seduced all of the bower-maidens and made the princess pregnant.'

'The princess is a worthy match for him,' says the old woman. Then she spoke to her daughter:

'Where are my foster-daughter's shoes?'[14]

She looked around and then said: 'That didn't turn out very well for me. It has been left behind at the hot spring, and it is now so late in the day that the way there is impassable because of the troll-hauntings.'

'That's a bit of a misfortune,'[15] said the old woman, 'because those shoes were dwarf-smithed, and it is their nature that they will never be able to get worn out, but she will never be able to wear another shoe, and she will now have to go with one foot bare.'

---

witness which contains the phrase, is equally legitimate, as it may simply be interpreted as an understatement on Silven's part, with the sense 'that's a bit of a misfortune'.

'Sökumzt ekki um það, fóstra mín,' segir hún, 'en þann einn skal ég mann eiga, að mér færir aptur skóinn.'

Og síðan geingu þær til sængur, en Vilmundur fór burt og kom seint heim. Þótti honum undarligur fyrirburður þessi, en ekki gat hann um þetta, hvorki fyrir kalli né kellingu, en minna gat hann sofið síðan en áður.

9. Kall átti einn grip, er honum þótti betri en allt annað. Það var ein geit. Hana kallaði hann Gæfu. Hún var stór sem naut og hafði fjóra spena sem kýr. Það brázt alldrei, að hún átti þrjú kið hvert ár, og var honum mikill bústyrkur að henni.

Það var einn tíma, að Vilmundur fann eigi geitina. Kall bað hann leita víðara. Vilmundur bjózt þá til ferðar. Hann var í bjarnskinnsstakki, rauðum loðnum, og saumaður með miklum hagleik, digurt silfurbelti hafði hann um sig, og á stóran saxkníf, búinn silfri, otursskinnskuf á höfði, og var slegin um silfurgjörð, hárið gult sem silki, og lá niður á herðum honum, og hrökk sem lokaspónn, breiðöxi mikla silfurrekna í hendi, er faðir hans hafði gefið honum. Kelling kom þá út og mællti:

'Hvert ætla þú nú að fara, Vilmundur?' sagði hún.

'Ég ætla að leita að Gæfu,' kvað hann.[16]

'Sjalldan hefur þú meir vandað búning þinn en svo mikið,' sagði hún.

'Ég mun nú ei fyrr heim koma en finn Gæfu,' kvað Vilmundur.

'Vel væri þá,' sagði hún, 'ef svo yrði.'

Síðan bað hann vel lifa föður sinn og móður og gékk burt á skóginn. En er hann hafði kannað þær leitir, sem hann var vanur, þá var framorðið mjög. Og lagðizt hann til svefns í hellisskúta einum, og svaf þar um nóttina. En um morguninn, er hann vaknar, var komin á þoka svo myrk, að hann sá hvergi frá sér. Gékk hann þa um skóginn og villtizt, og vissi ei hvar hann fór. Gékk hann svo allan þann dag, og annan til kvöllds, og var þokan æ því myrkvari.

Hann var nú kominn að hömrum nokkrum. Og þóttizt hann þá heyra mannamál alla vega fyrir sér, og allra kvikinda læti. Bergið var ýmsa vega litt, bæði hvítt og blátt, rautt og gult, og svo slétt sem skafið væri, en ei mátti hann sjá fyrir þokunni, hversu hátt var upp á bjargið. En einn veg heyrði hann upp í loptið mannamálið sem annars staðar.

En því næst, kom hann þar sem miklar dyr voru á bjarginu, og voru þar opnar, þar var fyrir hurð stór með járnlokum. Undrazt hann þetta mjög

---

[16] Apart from the literal meaning of 'to look for Gæfa', the phrase also means 'to search for fortune'. The pun on Gæfa's name is maintained at every subsequent point in the saga at which the word is used.

'Let's not blame each other for that, foster-mother,' she says, 'but the man who brings me back my shoe is the only man I'll marry.'

Afterwards they went to sleep, but Vilmundur departed and arrived home late. This vision seemed strange to him, but he did not speak about it to either his father or his mother, and he got less sleep after it than he had before.

9. The peasant had a treasure that he thought to be better than everything else. It was a nanny goat, and he called her Gæfa [Fortune]. She was as large as an ox and had four teats like a cow. She had three kids every year without fail, and she was a great domestic asset for the peasant.

One time, Vilmundur could not find the goat. His father bade him look further. Vilmundur prepared himself for his journey. He wore a bearskin coat, red and furry and sewn with great skill; around him he had a thick silver belt with a large dagger adorned with silver, on his head an otterskin cowl with a silver band around it, his silken gold hair, curly as plane-shavings, reaching down to his shoulders. In his hand was a great broadaxe mounted with silver, which his father had given him. His mother came out and said:

'Where do you intend to go now, Vilmundur?'

'I intend to look for Gæfa,' he said.[16]

'You've seldom paid more attention to your attire than now.'

'I won't return home before I find Gæfa,' Vilmundur said.

'It would be good,' she said, 'if that happened.'

Afterwards he bade his father and mother farewell and walked away into the forest. But by the time he had searched the places he was used to, it was very late, and he lay down to sleep in a jutting cave, spending the night there. In the morning when he awakens, there was such a dense fog that he could not see anything in front of himself. He walked through the forest and lost his way, not knowing where he went. He walked in this way for the entire day and until the evening of the second day, and the fog grew ever thicker.

Now he arrived at a steep cliff. He thought that he heard the voices of humans and noises of all kinds of creatures all around him. The cliff was coloured in various ways, both white and black, red and gold, and it was as smooth as if it had been scraped. He could not see how high the cliff was through the fog, but he heard the human voices up in the air as from other directions.

Next he came to a great doorway in the cliff, in which stood a great door with iron locks. It was open. He marvels greatly at that, but entered

og gékk þó inn um hliðið. Sér hann þá braut eina breiða. Hann geingur eptir henni, þar til að fyrir varð garður mikill og grind í hliðinu. Hún var ólæst. Hann hratt upp grindinni og gékk í garðinn. Þá kómu að honum fjóra menn, og mællti einn til hans:
'Þú hinn vondi gaur,' sagði hann, 'hver gaf þér orlof til að ganga hér inn með vopnum á náttartíma, og fá mér öxina.'
Vilmundur kunni þá öngvu að svara, en fékk honum öxina. Hann reiddi hana upp, og vill færa í höfuð Vilmundi. Vilmundur hleypur nú undir hann, og rekur hann niður fall svo mikið að öxin féll úr hendi honum. Einn af þeim rak staur svo mikinn um herðar Vilmundi, en Vilmundur greip í fætur þeim, sem hann hafði féllt, og sló með tvö, svo að þeir féllu, og stóð annar alldrei upp, en þeim varð harðkeypt, sem hann héllt á.

10. Vilmundur sér nú eitt mikið hús og fagurt, og þangað gékk hann. Þar sá hann ganga tólf menn, og báru silfurdiska í höndum sér. Vilmundur gékk eptir þeim. Þá var hrundið upp aptur hurðinni skjótara en hann varði, sem fyrir innan var, og féll hann undan inn aptur á gólfið öfugur. Vilmundur gékk nú inn, og sá þar sitja meir en fjórutigi meyja. Þær höfðu allar bjart hár, og gullband um höfuð. Ein bar langt af öðrum, og sat hún í miðið. Ekki þóttizt Vilmundur vita, við hver bragð hann var um kominn, en flestir þeir sem inni voru óttuðuzt Vilmund. Þjónustusveinar spurðu, hvort þeir skylldu ei kalla á menn að gjöra vart við þennan mann hinn mikla. Kongsdóttir svarar:
'Meinlauss er oss hann, og munum vér ekki við hann eiga. En ef hann vill annað en gott, þá mun þess kostur.'
En þeir sögðu það vogun mikla. Þá mællti kongsdóttir:
'Þú hinn mikli maður,' sagði hún, 'sit niður og fá þér mat, ellegar vertu burt úr vorri skemmu, og gjör oss öngva raun í hérvist þinni.'
Hann gékk þangað sem kongsdóttir sat, og settizt á stólinn fyrir framan borðið, og tók til matar. En þó hann hefði leingi matarlaus verið, þá fór hann artugliga að öllu. En er máltíð var lokið, mællti kongsdóttir:
'Þú hinn mikli maður,' kvað hún, 'gjör annathvort, far að sofa, eður gakk burt úr skemmunni.'
Hann sá eina sæng á miðju hallargólfi. Þangað gékk hann og legzt í hana. Kongsdóttir vill láta draga af honum klæðin, en hann villdi það ekki. Töluðu þær stelpurnar þá um með sér, að þessi maður mundi vera fífl eður illmenni nokkuð. Kongsdóttir kvaðzt ætla að óvanur mundi fjölmenni, og bað öngvan til hans leggja og lá hann þar um nóttina og sofnaði skjótt.

through the gate nonetheless. He sees a broad path, and he follows it until he came to a large enclosure with a gate in the doorway, which was unlocked. He pushed open the gate and walked into the enclosure. Four men approached him, and one of them spoke to him.

'You, wicked scoundrel,' he said, 'who gave you permission to enter here so armed at night? Give me the axe!'

Vilmundur did not know how to respond, so he gave him the axe. The man raised it up, wishing to strike Vilmundur on the head. Vilmundur runs under him and throws him down so hard that the axe fell from his hand. One of the men drove a large stake at his shoulders, but Vilmundur grabbed the legs of the man he had killed, and with him he struck the other two so that they fell; one of them never stood up again, and the one he was holding paid dearly.

10. Then Vilmundur sees a large and beautiful house, and he walked up to it. He saw twelve men walking there bearing silver dishes in their hands, and he followed them. The door was pushed open quicker than the man inside expected, and he fell backwards onto the floor. And when Vilmundur entered, he saw more than forty maidens sitting there. All of them had bright hair and golden bands around their heads. One far surpassed the others, and she sat in the middle. Vilmundur did not know what scheme he had come upon, but most of those inside were afraid of him. The serving-boys asked whether or not they should call on people to make this large man's presence known. The princess answers:

'He is harmless to us, and we will not fight with him. But if he intends something other than goodwill, then that will be a possibility.'

They said that that was very daring. Then the princess said:

'You, big fellow, sit down and have some food, or else begone from our bower and make no trouble for us during your stay here.'

He went to where the princess sat, set himself down on a chair in front of the table, and began to eat. And though he had been without food for a long time, he acted with propriety in every way. When the meal was over, the princess said:

'You, big fellow, either go to sleep or leave the bower.'

He saw a bed in the middle of the hall-floor, walked over to it and lay down in it. The princess wishes to have his clothes pulled off, but he did not want that. The girls then said amongst themselves that this man might be an oaf or a ruffian of some kind. The princess said that she thought that he was unaccustomed to being among a crowd, and asked that no one mind him. He quickly fell asleep and lay there for the night.

Um morguninn kom kongsdóttir til sængrinnar og vakti hann og bað hann upp standa, og verða í burtu þaðan, 'því að það verður bani þinn, ef menn sjá þig hér.'

'Seg mér fyrst,' segir hann, 'þat mér þykir miklu varða. Hvort ertu maður eður tröll, eður álfkona, eður hvar er ég kominn, eður hvað heitir þú?'

Hún brosti að og mællti: 'Þykir þér ég tröllslig vera?'

'Ekki veit ég það,' segir hann, 'ég hefi ekki tröll séð og eða álfa.'

'Gullbrá heiti ég,' segir hún, 'og er ég dóttir kongs þess, er hér ræður fyrir, og veit ég, að honum mun illa líka, ef hann veit, að þú hefir hér verið.'

'Heyrt hefi ég kong nefndan,' segir hann, 'en ekki veit ég hvað það er, því að ég hefi eigi menn séð fyrir utan föður minn og móður.'

'Hvað heitir faðir þinn,' segir hún, 'eður hvar áttu heima?'

'Faðir minn býr í einum dal langt í burt heðan,' segir hann, 'hann heitir Sviði.'

'Hvert skalltu fara?' segir jungfrúin.

'Ég leita að Gæfu,' segir hann.

En frúin brosti og mælti: 'Væntir þú hennar hér?' segir hún, 'eður hvað er það?'

'Það er geit föður míns,' segir hann, 'með þremur kiðum.'

'Ekki hefir hún hér komið,' segir hún, 'og skalltu flýta þér burt,' segir hún, 'og vera eigi fundinn hér.'

'Það skal vera,' segir hann, 'en þó vil ég segja þér draum minn áður. Ég þóttumzt hér vera sem nú er ég kominn. Ég þóttumzt sjá að landinu sigla skip mörg. Þar óð upp af einn gölltur. Hann var mikill og illiligur. Hann hafði rana og rótaði öllu. Eptir honum runnu mörg svín, og létu öll grimmiliga, en af landinu ofan rann í móti einn rauðkinnur, svo fagurt dýr, að ég sá eigi fegra. Það hljóp í mót gelltinum, og áttuzt þeir við harðan leik, en svo kom, að göllturinn lagði undir björninn. Var þá fólkið allt hrætt og flýði. Þótti mér þú koma þar, sem ég var. Þóttumzt ég taka þig upp undir bjálfa minn, og réðumzt ég síðan mót gelltinum, og vaknaði ég þá.'

'Mikill þykir mér draumur þinn,' segir hún, 'og þætti mér ekki ólíkligt, að þú mundir verða mér að gagni. Og ef þú staðfestizt hér hjá föður mínum, þá vitja þú mín til þeirra hluta, sem þú þarft.'

Síðan klæðir Vilmundur sig, og biður þær allar vel lifa. Geingur síðan út af turninum. Var þá komið fagurt veður og sólskin bjart.

11. Nú litazt Vilmundur um. Sér hann nú turna borgarinnar, er sólin skín á, og sýnizt honum við gull glóa. Ekki vissi hann hvar hann hafði inngeingið

In the morning the princess came to his bed and woke him, telling him to get up and be on his way, 'because it will be the death of you if people see you here.'

'Tell me first,' he says, 'something which seems of great importance to me: are you a human or a troll or an elf-lady? And what place have I come to? And what are you called?'

She smiled at that and said: 'Do I seem troll-like to you?'

'I don't know,' he says,' I've never seen trolls or elves.'

'I'm called Gullbrá,' she says, 'and I'm the daughter of the king who rules here. I know that it would displease him if he knew that you'd been here.'

'I've heard of the word "king",' he says, 'but I don't know what that is, because I haven't seen people before, apart from my father and mother.'

'What's your father called,' she says, 'and where is your home?'

'My father lives in a valley far from here,' he says, 'and he's called Sviði.'

'Where are you going?' says the young lady.

'I'm looking for Gæfa,' he says.

The lady smiled and said: 'Do you expect to find it here? What is it?'

'She's my father's she-goat,' he says, 'and she has three kids.'

'She hasn't come here,' she says, 'and you must hurry yourself away and not be found here.'

'So I shall,' he says, 'though first I wish to tell you of my dream. It seemed that I was here, exactly where I am now. I thought I saw many ships sailing towards the land. From them, a boar waded ashore, large and evil-looking, and it was wrecking everything with its snout. Many swine ran behind it, and they all acted fiercely. But from the land, a red bear charged against them, and I have never seen an animal more handsome. It charged against the boar, and they fought a hard battle, but eventually the boar laid the bear low. Then all the people were afraid and fled. You seemed to me to come to where I was, and I seemed to take you under my skin-coat, and we turned against the boar—and then I woke up.'

'Your dream seems significant to me,' she says, 'and it doesn't seem unlikely that you might become useful to me. Should you take up residence here with my father, call on me for anything you need.'

Afterwards, Vilmundur gets dressed, bids all the ladies farewell, and departs from the tower. The weather was beautiful and the sunshine bright.

11. Now Vilmundur looks around. He sees the towers of the city, on which the sun shines, and they seem to him to glitter with gold. He did not know

um kvölldið. Hann sér nú eitt hús, hvar rýkur, og geingur þangað. Þar eru inni margir menn, og katlar uppi, og slátur í soðið. Hann geingur innar yfir elldinn. Eingi maður leggur til hans. Hann sezt niður á einn knakk. Því næst kemur fram ein kona. Hún er í klæðum slitnum öllum. Hún grípur til hans með miklu afli og sviptir honum burt af knakkinum, svo hann liggur fallinn við öskuna, og nú grípur hann um hennar hönd og kreistir svo fast, að blóð stökk undan hverjum nagli. Hann tók um hennar háls og kreisti, svo vatn flaut um bæði hennar augu, og nú lítur hann hennar ásjónu og þykir mjög lík þeirri, sem hann sá í steininum, sleppir nú henni og stendur upp, og geingir burt úr steikarahúsinu.

Hann sér þá, hvar margir menn ganga inn í eitt hús, og þar geingur hann eptir. Kemur í eitt vegligt herbergi og sér þar sitja marga menn, og skilur hann af tilvísan kongsdóttur, að það muni kongurinn vera, sem allir lúta til. Matur var á borðum um alla höllina. Hann nemur staðar á gólfinu innarliga. Eingi maður leggur til hans. Kongur mællti þá við skutilsveininn, að hann skylldi gefa honum að drekka og biðja hann fá sér mat einshvers staðar í höllinni. Sveinninn gjörði sem kongurinn bað. Vilmundur sér, hvar einn stóll stendur eigi allfjarri sæti kongsins, og þar sezt hann niður, og var borinn matur fyrir hann. Hann neytti vel matar, og át eigi minna en fjórir riddarar. Margir hlógu að honum. Kongur mællti til hans:

'Hvert er nafn þitt, hinn mikli maður,' segir hann, 'eður hvaðan ertu kominn?'

'Vilmundur heiti ég,' segir hann, 'en ég er kominn frá föður mínum og móður.'

'Svo eru flestir,' segir kongur, 'eður hvert villtu fara, og þú ert vænn maður.'

'Ég leita að Gæfu,' segir Vilmundur.

'Feingið hafa þeir gæfu,' segir kongur, 'sem eigi eru mannvænligri en þú, eður sér þú hana nokkuð hér?'[17]

'Ekki,' segir Vilmundur, 'eður hefir hún ekki komið hér, svo að þér vitið?'

'Ég veit ei, hvað þú kallar gæfu,' segir kongur.

'Það er geit föður míns með þremur kiðum,' segir hann.

Þá hlógu allir menn í höllunni og sögðu, að þetta væri fífl, en kongur kvaðzt eigi það ætla, 'en vera má, að hann sé sjalldan vanur mönnum.'

Þessu næst kom maður í höllina, mikill vexti og mjög ósvipligur, og var þar kominn Ruddi. Hann mællti til kongs:

---

[17] The final sentence in this line of dialogue may be out of place (Olsson 1949, 14), but it appears there in all three extant medieval manuscripts. It seems a better fit in the king's next line.

where he had entered the previous evening. Then he sees a house which is emitting smoke, and walks up to it. Inside there are many people and standing pots, in which offal is being boiled. He walks farther inside, past the fire. No one pays him any attention. He sits down on a stool.

Next, a woman comes forth. She is dressed in utterly ragged clothes. She grabs him with tremendous strength and flings him away from the stool, so that he falls down into the pile of ashes. Then he grips her hand and crushes it so tightly that blood spurts from under each nail. He grasped her neck and squeezed it so that water streamed from both her eyes. Then he looks upon her face and thinks that it greatly resembles the one he saw in the stone. He lets go of her, stands up, and departs from the kitchen.

Then he sees many men going into a house, and he follows them in. He enters a splendid room, and sees many men sitting there, and he discerns from the princess' instructions that it would be the king to whom they are all bowing. Food was on tables throughout the whole hall. He stops on the floor, far inside. No one pays him any attention. Then the king said to a cup-bearer that he must give the man a drink and invite him to have some food somewhere in the hall. The boy did as the king instructed. Vilmundur sees a chair standing not too far from the king's seat, and he sits himself down there and food was brought before him. He tucked in with relish, eating no less than the portions of four knights. Many men laughed at him. The king spoke to him:

'What is your name, big fellow? And where have you come from?'

'I'm called Vilmundur,' he says, 'and I've come from my father and mother.'

'So do most,' says the king, 'but where are you intending to go? You're a promising man.'

'I'm looking for Gæfa,' says Vilmundur.

'Many men who aren't more promising than you have found *gæfa* [fortune],' says the king. 'Do you see it anywhere here?'[17]

'No,' says Vilmundur. 'Hasn't she come here that you know of?'

'I don't know what you call *gæfa*,' says the king.

'She's my father's goat, with three kids,' he says.

Everyone inside the hall laughed at that, and said that he was a fool. But the king declared that he did not think that, 'and it may be that he's hardly used to other people.'

Next, a man large in size and very evil-looking came into the hall: Ruddi had arrived. He said to the king:

'Mikla skamm hefir slammi sjá gjört yður, sem hér er kominn. Hann hefir sofið í nátt í turninum hjá dóttur þinni, og veit ég eigi, nema hann hafi gjört þar meira illbýli. Hann hefir og drepið tvö menn, þá sem garðinn áttu að verja, og veit ég, að hann mundi sitt höfuð missa, ef Hjarrandi væri heima.'

'Því geymdir þú svo illa garðinn?' segir kongur.

'Það er skyldazt, að ég skripta honum fyrir sína djörfung,' segir Ruddi.

'Það mundi gaman, að þið glímið,' segir kongur, 'en látum hefndina bíða Hjarranda.'

'Þá gangi mér at óskum,' segir Ruddi.

'Veitazt skal þér sú ósk,' sagði Vilmundur, 'og er ég til reiðu.'

Kongur segir, að þeir skylldu reyna úti í garðinum, þegar borðin eru upp tekin, 'því að þar mega fleiri gaman að hafa.'

Handleggjazt þeir nú þetta við, og geingur Ruddi nú í burt, en Hjarrandi kom nú heim við tólfta mann og gékk fyrir kong og kveður hann. Kongur fagnar honum vel, og biður hann sitja í hásæti hjá sér, og spyrr tíðinda, en Hjarrandi sagði slík sem voru. Hjarrandi spyrr, hver sá væri hinn mikli maður, er sæti í sæti hans.

'Sá maður er oss mjög ókunnigur,' segir kongur, 'því að hann kom hér í dag. Er oss sagt, að hann hafi sofið í nátt í turninum hjá systur þinni.'

'Það mætti kalla,' segir Hjarrandi, 'að hann væri nú vel að landsvist kominn, og skal honum það vel hegna.'

'Það mun nú mjög undir þér,' segir kongur, 'en þó hafa þeir Ruddi handlagið sig til fangs, og verðum vér að sjá þá skemmtun fyrst.'

Hjarrandi kvað hann þá heim kominn, 'því að þar munu jafnir á hæfazt.'[18]

'Eigi veit ég það,' segir kongur, 'en annaðhvort er um mann þetta, að hann er fífl, eður hann er eigi vanur hjá öðrum mönnum, en þó hygg ég, að hann þykizt nokkuð undir sér eiga fyrir afls sakir.'

Hjarrandi segir, að þetta mundi reynt verða.

12. Þegar borð voru upp tekin, geingur kongur í burt af höllunni og öll hirðin. Vilmundur gékk síðazt. Og er hann kemur út, sér hann, hvar kongur situr á stóli og Hjarrandi hjá honum, en hirðin stendur um kring um hann. Þar var völlur mjög staksteinóttur. Ruddi stóð á vellinum og var í fangastakki, og tók ofan á kné, og spyrr, hvar sá hrotti væri, er lagt hefir leik við sig. Vilmundur kom þá í garðinn.

---

[18] It is unclear whether Hjarrandi is saying that it is Ruddi or Vilmundur who would be right at home, but if the latter is the case, *heim kominn* 'come home' could be an ironic reference to Vilmundur's position as an outsider.

'Great shame has been brought on you by this oaf who has come here. He has slept the night in the tower with your daughter, and—I don't know—maybe he has violated even more there. He has also killed two men who were meant to be guarding the enclosure, and I know that he would lose his head if Hjarrandi were home.'

'Why did you watch the house so poorly?' says the king.

'It's my duty to punish him for his insolence,' says Ruddi.

'It would be fun if you two wrestled, but we will let the revenge wait for Hjarrandi,' says the king.

'Then things will be just as I wish,' says Ruddi.

'That wish will be granted you,' said Vilmundur, 'and I'm ready at hand.'

The king says that they should compete out in the courtyard, as soon as the tables are cleared 'because more people can enjoy it there.'

They shake hands on that, and then Ruddi departs. Hjarrandi returned home with eleven men, and he went before the king and greeted him. The king receives him well, invites him to sit on his high-seat beside him, and asks him for tidings. Hjarrandi told him such as there were. Hjarrandi asks who that big fellow who sat in his seat might be.

'That man is completely unknown to us,' says the king, 'because he came here today, and we were told that he had slept the night by your sister in the tower.'

'It might be said,' says Hjarrandi, 'that he's been living large, and he must be properly punished for that.'

'That matter lies in your power now,' the king says, 'but they, Ruddi and he, have shaken hands on a wrestling match, and we will watch that entertainment first.'

Hjarrandi said that he would be right at home then, 'because two equals will be battling there.'[18]

'I don't know about that,' says the king, 'but this man is one of two things: he's a fool, or he isn't used to being around other men, though I guess that he considers himself to be somewhat powerful because of his strength.'

Hjarrandi says that that would be put to the test.

12. As soon as the tables were cleared, the king and his whole retinue leave the hall. Vilmundur went last. When he comes outside, he sees where the king sits on a chair, with Hjarrandi beside him, while the retinue stand around him. There was a field full of stones. Ruddi stood on the field in his wrestling jerkin, which came down over his knees, and he asks where that lout who had agreed the contest with him might be. Then Vilmundur

Kongur segir, að Ruddi þættizt leingi bíða hans. Vilmundur sagðizt nú þar kominn og bað kong geyma öxi sína. Þá hlógu menn, en kongur spyrr, hvar þeir sæi þann, að betur væri till fallinn. Þeir sögðuzt eigi þann sjá, og kvoðu mikið um lítillæti hans. Vilmundur kastar klæðum og geingur fram á völlinn. Ruddi hleypur í mót honum, og rekur báða knefa fyrir brjóst honum af öllu afli. Vilmundur tók á mót sterkliga, og lagði hendurnar utan að handleggjunum á honum, og vatt honum á lopt sterkliga, og urðu þá sviptingar miklar með þeim, og varð flest upp að ganga, en hvar sem Ruddi tók á, þá blánaði allt undan, því að hann hafði fornskornar negl, en fangastakkurinn var svo seigur fyrir, að ekki gékk á hann.[19] Kongur og öll hirðin horfði á þenna leik, og þótti mikils vert um afl Vilmundar.

Þeir báruzt víða um völlinn, þar til að þeir kómu að þeim steini, sem sverðsegg var í greypt. Vilmundur mællti þá við Rudda:

'Skulum við leingi eiga leik þenna?'

'Þar til annar hvor fellur,' segir Ruddi.

'Gakk þú þá að betur,' segir Vilmundur.

Ruddi spyrnir nú við fótunum svo sterkliga, að hann veður jörðina í kné, en leggur svo hremsurnar um hrygg Vilmundi, að holdið gékk undan. Vilmundur tók hann þá upp á bringu sér, og gékk með hann að steininum, og keyrir hann niður á sverðseggina svo fast, að Rudda tók í sundur í miðju.

Gékk hann nú fyrir kong og héllt á fótahlutnum af Rudda, og sýndizt flestum hann þá grimmligur. Hjarrandi villdi þá upp standa og hefna Rudda, en kongur mællti:

'Eigi skulum vér níðazt á manni þessum, því lítill mannskaði var að Rudda, en ég vil eigi, að þú vogir þér undir heljarmann þenna,[20] en vitum fyrst, hvað hann kann íþrótta.'

Vilmundur kastar nú niður Rudda, en bað kong fá sér aptur öxi sína, 'því að mér lízt nú ekki trúliga á yður.'

Kongur mællti: 'Ertu svo búinn að fleirum íþróttum sem að afli?'

Vilmundur segir: 'Það sem ég kann íþrótta, þá hirði ég eigi, við hvern ég reyni. En ef þér vilið hafa líf mitt, þá megið þér prófa til, hvað ég hefi í móti að gera.'

---

[19] The phrase *forn skornar negl* literally means 'anciently cut nails'. In spite of this, the second half of the sentence presumably refers to Vilmundur being unable to pierce Ruddi's wrestling jerkin, because only Ruddi is actually said to be wearing one.

entered the courtyard. The king says that Ruddi felt he had waited a long time for him. Vilmundur said that he had now arrived, and he asked the king to guard his axe. Men laughed at that, but the king asks where they might see a man better suited for it. They said that they couldn't see one, and they praised his humility greatly.

Vilmundur casts off his clothes and walks forth onto the field. Ruddi charges at him and throws both his fists at Vilmundur's breast with all his strength. Vilmundur bore it staunchly, and, laying his hands on Ruddi's arms, he hoisted him powerfully into the air. Their struggle became great, and most things were thrown about. Wherever Ruddi took hold of him became completely bruised underneath, because he had uncut nails—but his wrestling jerkin was so tough that he could not pierce it.[19] The king and all his retinue watched the match and they took Vilmundur's strength very seriously.

The combatants hauled themselves far across the field, until they came to a stone in which a sword-edge sat in a groove. Then Vilmundur said to Ruddi:

'Will we be playing this game for a long time?'

'Until one of us falls,' says Ruddi.

'Come at me harder then,' says Vilmundur.

Ruddi then pushes so powerfully with his feet that he sinks to his knees into the earth, and he lays his clutches on Vilmundur's back so that the flesh was torn away. Vilmundur took hold of him, lifted him up to his chest, carried him to the stone and flings him down on the sword-edge so hard that Ruddi was split asunder in the middle.

Now Vilmundur went before the king holding the lower half of Ruddi, and to most present he seemed to be ferocious. Hjarrandi wished to rise up and avenge Ruddi, but the king said:

'We must not mistreat that man, because Ruddi's death was hardly a great loss, and I don't want you to pit yourself against that man of Hel,[20] but let's first find out what skills he knows.'

Vilmundur then casts Ruddi down, and asked the king if he could have his axe back, 'because now I don't feel safe among you.'

The king said: 'Are you as capable in any more skills as you are in your strength?'

Vilmundur says: 'Of the skills that I know, I don't care whom I'm tested against. And if you want to have my life, then you may test how I am able to counter this.'

---

[20] A *heljarmaður*, literally 'man of Hel', is someone with abnormal strength.

Hjarrandi spyrr nú, hversu hann kynni steini að kasta. Vilmundur bað hann taka steininn og ætla kastið. Hjarrandi tók upp þann stein, er stóð skippund,[21] og kastar í fyrstu tuttugu fet, og bað Vilmund eptir kasta. Hann gjörir svo, og kastar fram yfir tvær stikur.[22] Hjarrandi tók steininn í annað sinn, og kastar tólf fet og tuttugu. Vilmundur tók þá steininn, og kastar fram yfir þrjár stikur. Þá mællti kongur: 'Svo fór sem mig varði, að sjá maður er meiri fyrir sér en vér ætlum.' Hjarrandi reiðizt nú, og grípur steininn og sparir nú eigi af, og kastar fjörutigi fóta, og biður Vilmund eptir kasta. Hann gjörir svo, og snarar fram yfir fimm stikur. Hjarrandi vill þá eigi leingur til ganga.

13. Kongur biður Vilmund nú kasta svo langt sem hann getur. Vilmundur tók þá steininn og setur á fót sér, og kastar mannshæðar upp í hallarvegginn svo fast, að hann festi sig þar, og stendur þar enn í dag til sýnizt. Hjarrandi tók nú spjót eitt mikið og skýtur að einum steinstólpa, svo að upp gékk á falinn, og var það skot nírætt að leingd og hæð. Turn einn stóð upp á þeim stólpa mjög hár, og sat á ein dúfa. Vilmundur skaut því sama spjóti að fuglinum, og í gegnum hann, svo að hvorttveggja hrapaði ofan. Vilmundur rann þá í kringum höllina og henti stöngina og fuglinn á lopti. Hann skaut nú spjótinu í gegnum steinstólpann svo fast, að það stendur þar enn í dag, og má það þar sjá hver sem kemur.

Hjarrandi spyrr nú, hversu hann er búinn til sunds. Hann segizt sund bezt kunna af öllum íþróttum. Þeir ganga nú til vatns og kasta klæðum. Hjarrandi leggzt á vatnið og Vilmundur þegar eptir, og prófa þeir fyrst flýtissund, og þykir mönnum þar nærri um. Þar næst prófa þeir marga fimleika, og þykjazt menn eigi hafa séð vænni skemmtan. Hjarrandi leggzt nú að Vilmundi og færir hann í kaf, og voru þeir leingi niðri, og um síðir kómu þeir upp og voru mjög móðir. Vilmundur grípur nú til Hjarranda og færir hann í kaf, og voru nú svo leingi niðri, að öllum þótti líkligt, að þeir mundu dauðir, en vatnið vall af ókyrrleik. En er á leið daginn, þá kom Hjarrandi að landi og var svo stirður, að menn urðu að styðja hann, ef hann skylldi ganga, en til Vilmundar sá þeir ekki; og löngu síðar sá þeir mikinn boða rísa á vatninu. Þá kom Vilmundur upp og reisti upp einn hávan stein, og settizt á hann ofan og hvílldi sig þar á. En af tillögum vondra manna lét kongur leysa einn hvítabjörn, er geymdur var í grindum í borginni. Þeir siguðu honum á vatnið. Björninn lagðizt á vatnið og hristi sig grenjandi. Vilmundur

---

[21] A *skippund* is approximately 160 kilograms.
[22] Each *stika* is two ells, or approximately three feet.

Hjarrandi now asks whether he knew how to cast stones. Vilmundur told him to take the stone and make the throw. Hjarrandi took up a stone which weighed a *skippund*,[21] casts it twenty feet at first, and told Vilmundur to cast afterwards. He does so and casts it two *stikur* farther. Hjarrandi took the stone a second time and cast it thirty-two feet. Vilmundur took the stone and casts it three *stikur* farther.[22] Then the king said:

'It has gone as I suspected: there is more to this man than we thought.'

Hjarrandi grows angry. He grabs the stone, and, sparing no effort, casts it forty feet, telling Vilmundur to cast afterwards. He does so, flinging it five *stikur* farther. Hjarrandi doesn't want to continue any longer.

13. Now the king tells Vilmundur to cast as far as he can. Vilmundur took the stone, sets it on his foot, and kicked it the height of a man up into the wall of the hall, so hard that it became stuck there; it still stands there as proof today. Hjarrandi then took a large spear and throws it at a stone pillar, so that it pierced through to the shaft; the throw measured ninety fathoms high and long. On the pillar stood a very high tower, and on it sat a dove. Vilmundur threw the same spear at the bird and pierced it, so that they both hurtled downwards. Vilmundur then ran around the hall and caught the stick with the bird in mid-air. He then threw the spear through the stone pillar so hard that it still stands there today, and anyone who goes there can see it.

Hjarrandi now asks how well he can swim. He says that out of all skills, he knows best how to swim. Then they go to the water and take off their clothes. Hjarrandi starts to swim, with Vilmundur immediately after him, and first they test their sprint swimming, and it seems to the people there that they are almost equal to each other. Next they test many skills of agility, and the people think that they have never seen such fine entertainment. Hjarrandi then swims to Vilmundur and plunges him underwater. They stayed down for a long time, and a while later they surfaced and were very breathless. Vilmundur then grips Hjarrandi and plunges him underwater. They stayed down for such a long time that it seemed likely to everyone that they would be dead, but the water frothed restlessly. And as the day went on, Hjarrandi came to land, and he was so stiff that men had to support him so that he could walk. But they did not see Vilmundur. A long time afterwards, they saw a great surge rising from the water. Then Vilmundur surfaced. He raised a tall stone and sat upon it, resting himself there. But, on the advice of evil men, the king let loose a polar bear, which had been kept within a cage in the city. They drove it into the water. The bear swam into the water and shook itself, howling.

sér, að nú mun eigi vera setuefni, og kastar hann sér nú af steininum og leggzt í móti birninum og tekur höndum framan í granirnar á honum, og sviptazt þeir fast, og dregur björninn inn undir sig, og er hann nú ákafliga móður. Hann tekur nú sinn tygilkníf og stingur undir bóg dýrinu og inn til hjartans, og var það mikið áræðisverk að vinna að svo miklu kvikindi. En þegar björninn hefir banasár feingið, dettur hann dauður niður, því það er hans náttúra, að hann hefir eingi fjörbrot, en vatnið verður að blóði einu. Sá menn nú ekki til Vilmundar, en litlu síðar sá þeir, hvar hann flaut í blóðhrönninni. En er Hjarrandi sér það, leggzt hann á vatnið og að Vilmundi, og var hann svo máttdreginn, að hann gat sér ekki veitt, og lagðizt Hjarrandi til lands með hann, og var honum þá hjúkað í öllu og feingin góð klæði. Tók Vilmundr skjótt að nærazt. Eptir það bundu þeir Hjarrandi bræðralag, og var það allra manna mál, að eigi hefði vaskari maður komið í það land en Vilmundur var. En á meðan hann var nýkominn, var hann lítt í siðblendi við aðra menn, því jafnan er menn geingu til borða eður frá, þá varð að kalla á Vilmund, og því var hann jafnan einn og blandaðizt lítt við aðra menn, því var hann kallaður Vilmundur viðutan.

14. Það er nú þessu næst að segja, að Hjarrandi og Vilmundur fóru á skóg að veiða dýr og með þeim margir menn, og voru á skóginum, svo að vikum gegndi. Var þá enn sem optar, að Vilmundur fór einn saman og varð honum geingið víða. Kom hann nú á þá sömu sanda, sem fyrr hafði hann komið, og að þeim steini. Fór hann nú upp á steininn og sér slíka sýn og fyrr og hinar sömu konur. Hann heyrir nú, að þær talazt við og mællti hin gamla kona:
'Hvað var nú títt, fóstra mín, er þú fórt úr borginni?'
'Margt var tíðinda,' sagði hún, 'maður var þar kominn, sá er Vilmundur heitir, mikill vexti, en sterkur að afli, og þykir mönnum sem vera muni eldhúsfífl, en hann hefir unnið Hjarranda hvíðu, og eru þeir orðnir fóstbræður. En nú er ég fór heiman, sá menn skip að landi sigla, voru saman fimtán og tuttugu og voru flest drekar og drómundar,[23] og þótti mönnum sem þar mundi komin einnhver biðill Gullbrár, en Hjarrandi var nú á skógi og þeir Vilmundur, og þótti mönnum sem berserkir mundu við landið komnir, því að blámenn sáuzt í liði þeirra,[24] og þykir mönnum sem nú muni Hjarrandi reyndur verða.'
Síðan laukzt aptur steinninn, en Vilmundur snýr í burt þaðan.

[23] A *drómundur* is a type of ship from the Mediterranean.
[24] *Blámenn*, literally 'black men' or 'blue men', was used in earlier literature to refer to Ethiopians, but in later romances such as *Vilmundar saga* the term had come to refer to a type of stock monstrous villain representing a form of threatening otherness.

Vilmundur sees that there will be no time to rest, and he throws himself from the stone and swims against the bear. He seizes its jowls from the front, and they wrestle hard. He drags the bear under himself, and by now he is desperately breathless. Then he takes his dagger and stabs under the beast's shoulder into its heart, and it was a very courageous deed to kill such a great creature. As soon as the bear has received its death-wound, it drops dead, because it is its nature not to have any death-throes. The water becomes like blood.

The people did not see Vilmundur, but after a little while, they saw where he floated on the blood-tide. And when Hjarrandi sees that, he swims into the water towards Vilmundur, who was so exhausted that he could not help himself, and he headed to land with him. He was then nursed in all ways and brought good clothes. Vilmundur started to recover immediately. After that, Hjarrandi and Vilmundur swore an oath of foster-brothership, and it was the consensus of everyone that a more valiant man than Vilmundur had never arrived in that country. But while he was a newcomer, he had little social interaction with other men, because often when men went to or from meals Vilmundur had to be called, but he was frequently alone and seldom mixed with other men. Because of this, he was called Vilmundur viðutan [the Outsider].

14. Next, it is to be told that Hjarrandi and Vilmundur went into the forest to hunt animals. Many men were with them, and they were in the forest for several weeks. Then, as usual, Vilmundur went away alone, and he walked a long way. He came upon the same sandy expanses as he had visited before, and to the same stone. He climbed up onto the stone and sees such a sight as before, with the same women. Then he hears them talking among themselves, and the old woman said:

'What news was there, my foster-daughter, when you left the city?'

'There were many great tidings,' she said. 'A man called Vilmundur had come there, large in size and mighty in strength, and it seemed to people as though he would be a kitchen-slouch, but he has defeated Hjarrandi hvíða, and they have become foster-brothers. And then when I was going home, people saw ships sailing to land. There were thirty-five ships, mostly dragon-ships and *drómundar*,[23] and it seemed to people that it would be a suitor come for Gullbrá. But Hjarrandi and Vilmundur were then in the forest, and it seemed to the people that berserks might have come to land, because *blámenn* were seen in their host;[24] and so it seems that Hjarrandi might now be tested.'

Afterwards the stone closed, and Vilmundur turns away from there.

15. Einnhvern dag voru menn úti staddir hjá kongsatsetunni. Þeir sá skip af hafi sigla. Þau voru stór með svörtum seglum. Þau ber skjótt að landi, og báru þeir tjöld af skipum. Þessu næst voru menn sendir frá ströndu og kómu fyrir kong. Sá hét Skjölldur, er fyrir þeim var. Hann kvaddi kong og mællti:

'Sá kongsson hefir sent mig til yðar, er Buris heitir. Hann er son Ródíans kongs í Blökumannalandi.[25] Hann er nú kominn fyrir yðrar hafnir með þeim erindum, að hann vill fá yðra dóttur, er Gullbrá heitir, því að hennar prýði fer nú víða um heiminn, og bað hann, að þér munduð vel gjöra og færa honum til sjóvarins yðra dóttur og semdið þið þar ykkarn kaupmála, því hann vill eigi ónáða sitt fólk að ganga heim til hallarinnar. En ef þér vilið eigi svo gera, þá tekur hann yðra dóttur með herfangi, en drepur yður sjálfa og eyðir yðvart ríki.'

Kongur mællti: 'Þetta mál kemur eigi svo mjög til mín, því að Hjarrandi, hennar bróðir, ræður hennar gipting, og væntir mig, að hann muni einhver svör gefa þér hér um.'

Skjölldur segir, að kongsson vill eigi leingi vera vonbiðill hennar, 'og megið þér svo til ætla, að þegar á morgin er yður vís ófriður, ef þér synið konunnar, og sitið í frið,' og geingur hann nú til skipa.

Hjarrandi kom nú heim af skóginum, og voru honum sögð þessi tíðindi, en hann bað þegar kveða við lúðra, og var liði safnað að nálægum byggðum, og var tíminn helldur stuttur, og var nú hark mikið í borginni, er hver bjó sig með sínum vopnum.

En að morgni dags kveða við lúðrar í búðum Buris, og lætur hann setja upp merki sitt, og var víða þakinn völlurinn af hans her, og voru flest blámenn og berserkir. Hjarrandi fór í móti með sínum her, og var það lítill her hjá her Buris. Ekki var Vilmundur enn af skóginum kominn, og þótti mönnum hann nú sanna nafn sitt og vera viðutan. Skjölldur bar merki Buris, og var hann bæði sterkur og stórhöggur. Hjarrandi gékk í gegnum lið Buris, og stóð ekki við honum. Skjölldur snýr nú í mót honum og leggur til hans með spjóti. Hann stökk í lopt upp, og lagði Skjölldur í jörðina og laut eptir. Hjarrandi leggur sverðið um hrygg honum og tók hann í sundur um þvert, og sverðið sökk í jörðina að höndum honum.

---

[25] Blökumannaland is probably Wallachia in modern-day Romania. There is another King Ródían with a connection to Blökumannaland, this time in *Egils saga einhenda ok Ásmundar berserkjabana*, another *fornaldarsaga* with a Russian setting. In that saga, Ródían is king of Tartaría (Tartary), another eastern kingdom, and he is killed by two brothers from Blökumannaland. Characters with similar

15. One day, people were standing outside near the king's residence. They saw ships sailing in from the sea. They were large, with black sails. They bear quickly to land, and the men carried tents off the ships. Next, men were sent from the beach, and they came before the king. The man leading them was called Skjölldur. He greeted the king and said:

'The prince called Buris has sent me to you. He is the son of King Ródían of Blökumannaland.[25] He has now come before your harbours with this errand: he wishes to marry the daughter of yours named Gullbrá, because news of her splendour has travelled far throughout the world. He also asked you to be so kind as to deliver your daughter to him by the sea, and settle the deal between the two of you there, because he does not wish to trouble his people to go to your hall. But if you do not agree to do this, he will take your daughter along with plundered goods, and he will kill you and lay waste to your kingdom.'

The king said: 'That decision doesn't fall so much to me, because her brother Hjarrandi will ordain her marriage, and I expect that he will give you some sort of answer about that.'

Skjölldur says that the prince will not wish to play the stalled suitor for long, 'and you can therefore expect that war will immediately be upon you tomorrow, if you refuse us the woman. Go in peace.' Then he goes to the ships.

Hjarrandi then came home from the forest, and these tidings were told to him. He ordered that the trumpets be sounded immediately, and an army was assembled from nearby settlements. The time was rather short, and there was a great tumult in the city as everyone prepared themselves with their weapons.

In the morning, the trumpets are sounded in Buris's camps, and he has his standard set up. The field was largely covered by his army, and they were mostly *blámenn* and berserks. Hjarrandi moved against him with his army, but it was a small host next to Buris's. Vilmundur had still not returned from the forest, and it seemed to people that he had proven his nickname and was indeed an outsider. Skjölldur carried Buris's standard, and he was both strong and a hard hitter. Hjarrandi charged through Buris's host, and no one stood against him. Skjölldur then turns towards him and tries to stab at him with his spear, but he leapt into the air, and Skjölldur struck down into the earth and stumbled forward. Hjarrandi swings his sword through his back and split him asunder across the middle, and the sword sank into the earth all the way up to his hands.

---

names also appear in *Elis saga ok Rósamundu*, *Jarlmanns saga ok Hermanns* and *Karlamagnus saga*; in the latter two, they are also kings.

Þá kom Buris mót Hjarranda, og hófu þeir sitt einvígi með svo stórum höggum, að sá þóttizt bezt hafa, sem first þeim var. Buris var svo magnaður, að hann bitu eigi járn. En hlífar hjugguzt af Hjarranda, og því báruzt sár á Hjarranda. Hann spennir nú sitt sverð tveim höndum og höggur til Buris. Það kom um þvert andlitið á jungkæranum, og brotnaði í honum nefið og tanngarðurinn hinn efri, og hrundu tennurnar allar í gras. Mæddi Hjarranda þá blóðrás, og féll hann með stórum sárum, og slær nú felmti miklum á fólkið.

16. Í þessu bili kemur Vilmundur heim til borgarinnar af skóginum, og var kongsdóttir komin á flótta og ætlaði að fela sig. Vilmundur spyrr nú, hvað um er, og kvoðuzt menn ætla, að Hjarrandi mundi dauður.

Vilmundur fór þá til bardagans, og voru þá allir komnir á flótta. Og er menn sá Vilmund, varð sá margur fullhugi, sem áður var hræddur, og tekzt nú bardaginn í öðru sinni. Var Vilmundur nú fremztur í fylkingunni. Buris sótti nú á mót honum og hjó til hans. Vilmundur brá við skilldinum, og klofnaði hann niður að mundriða, en sverðsoddurinn nam á honum ennið, og var þat lítið sár og blæddi mjög. Vilmundur snaraði svo fast skjölldinum, að Buris varð laust sverðið. Vilmundur hjó með tveim höndum til Buris með öxinni framan á bringuna, og varð svo mikið höggið, að Buris kiknaði við, en eigi beit. Vilmundur snýr þá öxinni og setti hamarinn við eyra á Buris, og mölbrotnaði í honum hausinn. Þá urðu menn hans felmsfullir, og brast flótti í liði þeirra, en Vilmundur og borgarmenn ellta þá til skipa, og geingu sumir á kaf, en sumir voru drepnir á landi, og gáfu eigi fyrri upp en allt það illþýði var drepið, svo að alldrei einn maður var eptir af hans mönnum, en það herfang, sem þeir feingu í gulli og silfri vopnum og klæðum, skipum og landtjölldum, var svo mikils vert, að þess kunni eingi marka tal.

Vilmundur kannar nú valinn og fann Hjarranda lífs og mjög sáran. Hann var nú heim borinn, og tók systir hans að græða hann, og var hann skjótt lífvænn. Vilmundur lét hreinsa borgina, en flytja hina dauðu á sjó út og sökkva til grunna. Líða nú tímar, þar til Hjarrandi var gróinn.

17. Vilmundur segir nú Hjarranda, að hann vill vitja föður síns. Hjarrandi bað hann svo gjöra. Vilmundur hittir nú Sviða og segir honum, hvað yfir hann hafi drifið, síðan þeir skilldu, og bauð honum að fara með sér og búa eigi leingur svo fjarri mönnum. Sviði þá það og sagði sér leiðazt í fásinninu. Fór hann nú með Vilmundi til kongs, og var hann

Then Buris advanced against Hjarrandi, and they conducted a duel with such mighty blows that the one who was furthest away from them thought himself best off. Buris was so ensorcelled that iron did not cut him. Hjarrandi's armour was hacked off, and so Hjarrandi was wounded. Hjarrandi then grabs his sword with both hands and strikes at Buris, and it flew across the young nobleman's face, breaking his nose and upper row of teeth and spilling all his teeth onto the grass. By then, Hjarrandi was exhausted from his loss of blood, and he fell with great wounds, and great fear now seizes the people.

16. At that moment, Vilmundur comes back to the city from the forest, and the princess had fled, intending to hide herself. Vilmundur asks what was going on, and people said that they thought that Hjarrandi was dead.

Then Vilmundur entered the battle. Everyone had taken to flight, but when they saw Vilmundur, each man who had previously been afraid became a brave hero, and the battle begins a second time. Vilmundur was now the foremost of the host. Then Buris advanced against him, and hewed at him. Vilmundur blocked with his shield, and it was cloven down to the shield-handle, but the sword-point stopped in his forehead, causing a small wound there, and lots of bleeding. Vilmundur twisted the shield so quickly that Buris dropped his sword. Vilmundur hewed two-handed with his axe before Buris' chest, and it was such a mighty blow that Buris fell to his knees, but it did not cut him. Vilmundur then twists the axe, set the head against Buris' ear and smashed his skull. Then his men became terrified, and flight broke out in their ranks. But Vilmundur and the townspeople chased them to the ships. Some started to swim, but some were killed on land, and Vilmundur and his men did not let up before all of that rabble were killed, so that not a single man from that troop was left alive afterwards. But the spoils, which they took in gold and silver, weapons and clothes, ships and tents, were so precious that no one could measure their worth.

Now Vilmundur searches the slain and found Hjarrandi alive, with severe wounds. He was borne home, and his sister set about healing him, and soon he started to recover. Vilmundur had the city cleared and the dead carried out to sea and sunk to the bottom. Time passes until Hjarrandi has recovered.

17. Now Vilmundur tells Hjarrandi that he wishes to visit his father, and Hjarrandi told him to do so. Vilmundur then meets with Sviði and tells him what has happened to him since they parted, inviting him to go with him and not live so far away from people any longer. Sviði accepted that and told him that he was tired of isolation. Then he went with Vilmundur to the king and was made

settur höfðingi yfir eitt mikið herað, og sá menn skjótt á, að hann kunni góðan setning bæði lands og laga, og var mikill styrkur að honum.

Nú tekur þar til, sem Kolur kryppa var á skóginum og gjörði margt illvirki og herjar á land kongs, brenndi bæði kastala og kauptún, en drepur menn og rænir fé. Kongur kemur að máli við Hjarranda og biður hann fara að Kol, og búazt þeir Vilmundur nú á skóginn og leituðu Kols og höfðu sextigi manna. Kolur hafði þá riðið í byggðina og brennt einn kastala og tekið mikið fé og reið nú aptur í skóginn með þrælum sínum. Koma þeir Hjarrandi nú á móti þeim, og slær þegar í bardaga. Sækir Kolur fast fram og hans menn, og voru þeir svo fjölkunnigir, að náliga bitu eigi vopn manna Hjarranda utan þeim Vilmundi. En er sókn var sem hörðuzt, kómu fram úr skóginum fimmtigi svína og sækja að mönnum Hjarranda og rífa þá til dauðs. En þó að þeir hyggi til þeirra, þá hrukku sverðin upp í móti. Var þessi atgangur bæði harður og hættligur. Þó féllu um síðir allir þrælar Kols og svo allir menn þeirra fóstbræðra. Þá voru eptir tíu svínin. Stökkur Kolur þá á skóginn. Báðir voru þeir Vilmundur og Hjarrandi sárir, en þó elltu þeir Kol til kastalans, og skilldi þar með þeim. Fóru þeir þá heim og voru mjög stirðir, en urðu þó snart heilir.

Nú safnar Kolur liði í annat sinn og fær tuttugu menn, og helldur hann sömu fram um sitt athæfi, og hvar verri en fyrr. Þeir fóstbræður fara á skóginn í öðru sinni að Kol og höfðu hundrað manna og verða varir við, að Kolur er farinn í byggðina. Ríða þeir að honum, og slær enn í bardaga með þeim. Er enn sem samt segi, að Kolur er stórhöggur, en deyfði eggjar fyrir mönnum Hjarranda. Koma þá fram svínin og sækja að þeim. En svo lyktazt leikur þessi, að allir féllu menn Hjarranda og svo Kols.

Vilmundur tekur þá að berjazt við svínin, en Hjarrandi við Kol. Hann höggur nú til Kols og ofan í skallan, sem honum var hægazt, en sverðið stökk í sundur og beit ekki. Kolur skók höfuðið og hjó til Hjarranda, en hann snerizt undan á hæli. Sverðið kom á kálfann og reist niður allan, og var það mikið sár. Hjarrandi greip í eyrat á Kol og rykkti af honum vangafillunni, svo að berar skinu við tennurnar. Kolur stökk þá í skóginn og flýði.

Vilmundur hafði þá drepið svínin öll nema gylltuna. Hún komzt á skóginn og hafði bitið af Vilmundi einn fingurinn, og skilldi svo með þeim, og segja þeir nú kongi, hvað í hafði gerzt, og þótti honum æ úr einum brunni bera um illsku Kols. En þegar Hjarrandi var gróinn, hafði hann mikinn hug á að hefna sín á Kol.

chieftain over a large district, and soon men saw that he knew the proper order of both land and laws. The land was much stronger for his presence.

Now the story is taken up where Kolur kryppa was in the forest, committing many crimes and harrying the king's realm, burning both castles and market-towns, and killing men and stealing livestock. The king discusses this with Hjarrandi, and he asks him to attack Kolur. Hjarrandi and Vilmundur prepare themselves to go into the forest with sixty men, and they searched for Kolur. Kolur had ridden into the settlement, burnt a castle and taken much plunder, and he was now riding back into the forest with his thralls. Now Hjarrandi's men advance against them, and the battle is immediately joined. Kolur and his men push forward hard, and they were so skilled in sorcery that the weapons of Hjarrandi's men, apart from those of Vilmundur and Hjarrandi, were almost unable to cut them. But when the fight was at its hardest, fifty swine burst forth out of the forest and attack Hjarrandi's men, tearing some to death. And though the men hewed at them, their swords were repelled. Their battle went both hard and dangerously, but in the end all of Kolur's thralls were finally felled, and so too were all of the foster-brothers' men. There were still ten swine left. Kolur then runs into the forest. Both Vilmundur and Hjarrandi were wounded, but nonetheless they pursued Kolur to his stronghold, and they were separated from him there. They went home, greatly exhausted, but they recovered quickly.

Now, for the second time, Kolur assembles a host. He gets twenty men and continues with his activities, but much worse than before. For the second time, the foster-brothers go into the forest to attack Kolur, with a hundred men. They become aware that Kolur has gone to the settlement, and they ride to him and the battle is joined again. It was still the case as was said before, that Kolur was a hard hitter, and he blunted the blades of Hjarrandi's men. Then the swine burst forth and attack them, and the contest ended with all of Hjarrandi and Kolur's men falling dead.

Then Vilmundur engages in combat with the swine, and Hjarrandi with Kolur. Hjarrandi had an easy chance and strikes at Kolur down onto his bald head, but the sword snapped asunder and did not cut him. Kolur shook his head and hewed at Hjarrandi, and he immediately spun away from it. The sword cut into his calf, slicing all the way down and causing a severe wound. Hjarrandi grabbed Kolur by the ear and wrenched the flesh off his cheek, so that the teeth shone bare. Kolur then ran into the forest in flight.

By that point, Vilmundur had killed all the swine except the sow. Having bitten off one of Vilmundur's fingers, she ran into the forest, and they parted thus. Now they tell the king what has happened, and it seemed to him that Kolur's wickedness was always drawn from the same well. And as soon as Hjarrandi was healed, he had a strong desire to avenge himself on Kolur.

18. Það var eina nátt, að Vilmundur vaknaði og var Hjarrandi á burtu. Hleypur hann nú á fætur og tekur vopn sín, fer nú á skóginn.

Og er hann kemur nær kastala Kols, sér hann á einni mýri, hvar þeir eigazt við, Hjarrandi og Kolur, og var gylltan komin í leikinn með Kol, og hafði Hjarrandi feingið þrjú sár, og brotið hafði hann sverð sitt, og nú fékk hann einn stóran stein, svo að fjórir menn mundu valla getað lypt. Hjarrandi kastar honum að Kol, og kom beint á tenn honum, svo að Kolur féll á bak aptur, og kom knakkinn á stein, og brotnaði hausinn í mola, og lauk svo ævi Kols.

Gylltan hljóp að Hjarranda svo hart, að hann féll til jarðar. Í því kom Vilmundur að og lagði til gylltunnar með spjóti, en hún skaut við sigginu, og stökk spjótið í sundur. Vilmundur greip þá á aptur fót hennar, og rykkir að sér svo fast, að kviðurinn rifnaði, en iðrin féllu niður úr henni. Hún hafði fest tennurnar framan í herklæðunum á brjósti Hjarranda og svo nær beininu, að hún reif af honum geirvörtuna, svo að berir skinu við bringuteinarnir á honum, því að Vilmundur kippti svo snöggt, að bæði var senn á lopti Hjarrandi og gylltan. Dó nú gylltan, en Hjarrandi var óvígur.

Í þessu bili fékk Vilmundur högg svo mikið um þverar herðarnar, að hann féll á kné báðum fótum. Snýzt hann þá við og sá, að þar er komin Sóley, vinkona Kols, og sækir hún nú að Vilmundi í ákafa, svo að það var leingi, að hann átti eigi annað að gjöra en verja sig. Sér hann nú, að eigi má í annarri hendi hafa við hana. Grípur hann nú í hennar hár og vefur því um hönd sér, en annarri hendi tekur hann sitt sax og setur á hennar háls, svo að af fauk höfuðið. Var hann nú bæði móður og stirður. Leggur hann nú Hjarranda á sinn skjölld og ber hann heim af skóginum og inn í garðinn Viðbjóð og bað Gullbrá lækna hann, en hann gékk inn í höllina og setti höfuð Sóleyjar á borð fyrir konginn alblóðugt og mællti svo:

'Nú er dauður Kolur kryppa, mágur þinn, hinn mesti spillvirkir, sem verið hefir, og tak nú við höfði hans frillu, og munu þessir spillvirkjar eigi leingur spilla ríki þínu.'

Kongur varð svo reiður við orð hans, að hann bað sína menn upp standa og drepa fól þetta, er svo mikla svívirðing hefir honum gjört að setja það höfuð á borð fyrir hann, er svo var háttað, 'því að þó að ég villda mína dóttur dauða fyrir sín illbrigði, þá má ég ei þá skamm þola, að hennar blóð renni yfir mín borð, svo sem það kalli á mig til hefndar eptir sig. Því skal Vilmundur eigi fyrir mín augu koma að svo búnu mínu lyndi.'

Menn voru eigi skjótir til að ráða að Vilmundi, og sneri hann burt úr höllunni og bað sinn svein taka sinn hest, og reið Vilmundur nú til síns

18. Vilmundur awoke one night, and Hjarrandi was gone. He leaps to his feet, takes his weapons, and goes into the forest. And when he comes near Kolur's stronghold, he sees Hjarrandi and Kolur fighting in a swamp, and the sow had joined the contest in support of Kolur. Hjarrandi had received three wounds and broken his sword, and he now picked up a stone so large that four men would hardly be able to lift it. Hjarrandi casts it at Kolur, and it flew straight into his teeth, so that Kolur fell backwards and hit the back of his head on a rock, smashing his skull into pieces. Thus ended Kolur's life.

The sow leapt at Hjarrandi so fiercely that he fell to the ground. At that moment, Vilmundur came forth and stabbed at the sow with his spear, but she deflected it with her hide and the spear snapped asunder. Vilmundur then grasped her by one of her back legs, and wrenches it towards him so hard that her belly ripped and her entrails fell out of her. But she had clamped her teeth through Hjarrandi's armour to his breast, so near to the bone that she ripped a nipple from him and the cartilage in his lower breast shone bare, because Vilmundur had jerked so suddenly that both Hjarrandi and the sow were thrown into the air at the same time. The sow then died, and Hjarrandi was left incapacitated.

At that same moment, Vilmundur received such a great blow across his shoulders that he fell onto both knees. He turns around and saw that Sóley, Kolur's lady-friend, has appeared. She now attacks Vilmundur so forcefully that for a long time he could do nothing but defend himself. He realises now that he cannot overcome her with just one hand. He grasps her hair and winds it around his hand, and with his other hand he takes his dagger and thrusts it into her neck so that her head flew off. By then he was both stiff and exhausted. He lays Hjarrandi on his shield and bears him home, out of the forest and into the enclosure named Viðbjóður, asking Gullbrá to heal him. Then he went into the hall, and set the bloodied head of Sóley on the king's table, saying:

'Kolur kryppa, your son-in-law and the greatest troublemaker who has lived, is now dead. Receive now the head of his mistress. These troublemakers will no longer harm your kingdom.'

The king grew so angry at his words that he ordered his men to stand up and kill the fool who had so greatly dishonoured him by setting that head on the table before him in such a way, 'for although I wanted my daughter dead because of her misdeeds, I cannot endure the shame of her blood running over my tables, as if it urges me to avenge it. Because of this disgrace, Vilmundur must never again come into my sight.'

His men were not quick to attack Vilmundur, and he departed from the hall and ordered his squire to fetch his horse. Then Vilmundur rode to

föður og segir honum sem komið er, en Sviði segir, að kongur hefði mikið til síns máls, og það væri ofraun að setja slíkt höfuð á borð fyrir kong.

Vilmundur dvelzt nú með föður sínum, og síðan tekur hann sér hesta og marga menn til fylgdar og fer í kastala þann, sem Kolur hafði átt, og voru þar allsnægtir, bæði vist og vín, gull og gersimar, og dvelzt Vilmundur þar nú nokkura hríð.

Hjarrandi grær skjótt sára sinna. En er þeir feðgar finnazt, ávítaði Hjarrandi föður sinn, hversu hann hafði skilið við Vilmund. En kongur segir, að það var svo mikil ofraun, að hann gjörði, að það var eigi um beranda, en Hjarrandi segir, að hann mundi verða sárbeitur í sektinni, ef hann vill öðru til sín slá en góðu, og skilldu þeir feðgar að svo mælltu.

19. Eitt sinn gékk Vilmundur frá kastala sínum, því að honum þótti daufligt, síðan þeir Hjarrandi skilldu. Gékk hann nú til laugar þeirrar, sem hann hafði fyrri til komið. Sér hann nú, hvar þrjár konur ganga frá lauginni og til steinsins. Hann fór upp á steininn að heyra, hvað þær tala. Þá tók hin gamla kona til orða:

'Hvað er nú í fréttum, fóstra mín?' segir hún, 'og hefir nú langt verið, síðan þú fannt mig.'

'Margt hefir nú til nýlundu borið,' sagði hin, 'er það fyrst, að drepinn er Kolur kryppa og svo Öskubuska, kona hans, og má það heita nauðsynjaverk.'

'Hver vann það?' segir kelling.

'Hjarrandi og Vilmundur,' sagði hún, 'og varð Hjarrandi bana maður Kols, og lá þó sem næst, að Hjarrandi mundi þar ganga frá sínu lífi, ef Vilmundur hefði eigi hjálpað honum, en Vilmundur banaði frú Öskubusku, og hann drap þá grimmu gylltu, sem menn ætluðu, að alldrei mundi sigruð verða, og víst veit ég það, að vaskari maður mun eigi finnazt en Vilmundur er, en eigi fékk hann þau laun, sem mér þótti hann til vinna, því að kongur gjörði hann útlægan.'

'Hvað bar þar til?' segir kelling.

Hún segir henni nú sem farið hafði með þeim.

'Víst þætti mér Vilmundur gjöra kongi ofraun,' segir kelling, 'ef svo hefði verið sem kongur hugði. En nú er því betur, að það er eigi, eður hversu leingi skalltu þanninn leynazt, fóstra mín?'

'Eigi er mér annt um,' segir hún, 'að opinbera mig. Það þótti mér enn tíðindavænligt, fóstra mín,' segir hún, 'að vér sám skip að landi sigla tuttugu. Þau voru skrautlig og vel búin, og einn dreki svo vænn, að öngvan his father and tells him what has happened. Sviði says that the king had good reason for his decree, and that it was too severe an ordeal to place such a head on the table before the king.

Now Vilmundur stays with his father, and afterwards he takes his horse and many men in a retinue and goes to the stronghold that Kolur had owned. There was an abundance of everything, both food and wine, gold and treasures. Vilmundur stays there for some time.

Hjarrandi recovers quickly from his wounds, and when he and his father meet, Hjarrandi rebuked his father over how he had parted with Vilmundur. But the king says that it had been so severe an ordeal that he had caused that it could not be tolerated. Hjarrandi says that Vilmundur would become destructive in his outlawry if he wished to do anything other than good. Father and son parted with those words.

19. One time, Vilmundur went out from his stronghold, because things had seemed dull to him since he and Hjarrandi parted. He went to the hot spring that he had visited before. Now he sees three women walking from the spring to the stone. He climbed up onto the stone to hear what they are talking about. The old woman began to speak:

'What's there to report now, my foster-daughter? It's been a long time since you visited me.'

'Many curious things have happened,' she said, 'the first of which is that Kolur kryppa has been killed, and so has his wife Öskubuska. One might call that a necessary deed.'

'Who caused that?' asked the old woman.

'Hjarrandi and Vilmundur,' she said, 'and Hjarrandi was Kolur's killer, but it almost happened that Hjarrandi might have departed from life there if Vilmundur hadn't helped him. Vilmundur killed the woman Öskubuska, and he also killed the grim sow that people thought could never be defeated. And I know for certain that a braver man than Vilmundur can't be found. But he didn't receive the rewards that it seemed to me he'd earned, because the king had him outlawed.'

'What brought that about?' says the old woman.

She tells her what had happened between them.

'Vilmundur certainly seems to me to have caused too severe an ordeal for the king,' says the old woman, 'if it had gone as the king believed. But it's fortunate that it didn't. How long will you hide yourself in this way, my foster-daughter?'

'I'm not keen on revealing myself,' she says. 'Foster-mother, the fact that we saw twenty ships sailing to land seems to me to signify great tidings. They were splendid and well bedecked, and there was a dragon-ship

sá ég fyrr honum líkan, og þótti öllum sem þeir mundu langt að komnir, en fyrr fór ég af stað en ég vissa, hverir þeir voru.'

'Auðvitað mun það,' segir kelling, 'að þar mun kominn einnhver biðill Gullbrár.'

'Þá mun Hjarrandi verða reyndur,' kvað hin, 'og íþróttir hans, og stendur hann nú einn upp, er Vilmundur er eigi hjá honum.'

'Eigi veit ég, hvar til ætlar um metnað Hjarranda,' segir kelling, 'eður hvers Gullbrá verður auðið um giptingina. En þá þætti mér meira varða um þína gipting að vita hana góða, og betur þætti mér fallið, að Vilmundur ætti þig en Kolur, sem menn ætluðu að vera mundi.'

'Vel þatti mér sú kona gipt, sem Vilmundur ætti,' segir mærin, 'en skipazt ætla ég að þurfi með þeim föður mínum, áður en þeir drekka sáttir saman, en eigi villda ég það til vinna, þó ég ætti kosti að vera í kastalanum hjá Vilmundi, ef hann færi svo með sínu máli sem Kolur, en frétta munum vér nú fyrst, hvað til tíðinda ber heima.' Lykzt aptur gluggurinn, en Vilmundur fór til kastala síns, og hafði hann njósnarmenn í borginni að vita, hvað þar fór fram.

20. Balldvini er kongur nefndur. Hann réð fyrir Galicía. Hann var kvongaður og hafði feingið drottningu af dýrum ættum, og með henni átti hann tvö börn, einn vaskan son og væna dóttur. Hans son hét Guðifreyr.[26] Hann var vaskur maður og vel siðaður og umfram flesta menn að öllum íþróttum. Hann var svo vinsæll, að hver maður unni honum hugástum. Hans systir hét Rikiza. Hún var allra kvenna fríðuzt og mennt hverri mey betur á því landi. Kongur unni mikið börnum sínum.

Guðifreyr fór í hernað með miklu liði, og fór hann vel með hernaði sínum. Hann herjaði um austurveginn.[27] Hann hafði spurn af Gullbrá, og var honum mikið sagt af hennar vænleik. Frétt hafði hann og ummæli Hjarranda um gipting hennar, og því gjörir hann ferð sína til Hólmgarðs.

Kongsmenn voru úti, þá er skipin siglldu að höfnum, og fannzt mönnum mikið um sigling þeirra. Þeir höfðu tuttugu langskip og einn dreka, og var allur gulli búinn fyrir ofan sjó. Þóttuzt menn eigi hafa séð vænni sigling og skip eður meir vandaðan reiðskap, því að allir streingir voru sem á gull eitt sæi, en seglin voru stöfuð með allra

---

[26] 'Guðifreyr' is an uncommon name in Norse literature. Interestingly, there is a Galician chieftain with that name in the early thirteenth-century *Orkneyinga saga*.

[27] In Old Norse literature, the term *austurvegur* refers to the maritime route east along the Baltic, through the Gulf of Finland, and into Russia. See Section 2d of the introduction.

so fine that I've never seen its like before, and it seemed to everyone that they were coming from afar; but I left that place before I could discover who they were.'

'It's obvious that a suitor has come for Gullbrá,' the old woman says.

'Then Hjarrandi and his skills will be tested,' the young lady said. 'He now stands alone, as Vilmundur isn't beside him.'

'I don't know what's in store for Hjarrandi's honour, or how it will turn out for Gullbrá regarding her marriage,' says the old woman. 'But it seems more important to me that your marriage turns out well. It seems more fitting to me that Vilmundur should marry you than Kolur, whom people thought it would be.'

'I think that the woman whom Vilmundur marries would wed well,' says the maiden, 'but I think things would have to change between him and my father before they drink together in reconciliation. And I don't want to work towards that—though I'd have the choice of being in the stronghold beside Vilmundur—if he were to proceed in the same way as Kolur. But first we should see what will come to pass at home.' The window closes. Vilmundur went to his stronghold, and he had spies in the city to tell him what went on there.

20. There was a king was called Balldvini, and he ruled over Galicia. He was married to a queen of noble heritage, and he had two children with her, a valiant son and a fair daughter. His son was called Guðifreyr.[26] He was a valiant and well-mannered man, and superior to most men in all skills. He was so popular that every man loved him wholeheartedly. His sister was called Rikiza, and she was the fairest of all women, and more cultured than every woman in that land. The king loved both his children greatly.

Guðifreyr went to war with a large host, and things went well with his forays. He harried across the east-way.[27] He heard of Gullbrá, and he was told a great deal about her beauty. He had also learned of Hjarrandi's decree regarding her marriage, and for this reason he makes his way to Hólmgarður.

The king's men were outside when the ships sailed into the harbour, and many of them thought highly of their sailing. They had twenty longships and a dragon-ship which was completely covered with gold above the waterline. The people thought that they had never seen sailing or ships more beautiful, or masts more elaborate, because all the ropes appeared as though one were looking at gold, and the sails were striped with all

handa vefjum, pell og silki og guðvef.²⁸ Þessir menn helldu til hafna og báru tjölld á land, og fannzt mönnum þá eigi minna til, hversu hæverskliga þeir hlóðu sínum seglum eður hversu mikill ljómi yfir kom, þá þeir reistu sín landtjölld, því að alla vega lýsti af þeim karbunkuli, sem settir voru í þá knappa með gull gjöra, sem stóðu upp af þeirra tjölldum.

Þeir segja nú kongi, að þar munu komnir tignir menn af öðrum löndum. Þá lætur hann forvitnazt um, hverir þessir voru, og sendir Hjarranda til sjóvar. En er hann kom nærri landtjölldunum, þá geingu margir menn í móti honum, og þar sá hann einn mann, þann sem langt bar af öllum. Hjarrandi heilsar þeim hæverskliga og þeir honum á móti. Hann spyrr, hver höfðingi þeirra er. Þessi hinn fríði maður mællti:

'Guðifreyr heiti ég,' segir hann, 'og er ég son Balldvina kongs af Galicía.'

'Oss forvitnar,' segir Hjarrandi, 'hvert erindi þér eigið í vort land með svo mikinn her.'

Guðifreyr segir: 'Oss þykir gott að vera viðbúnir, ef nokkur vill vont, en vor liðsfjölldi skal yður ekki að meini koma, því að vér viljum hér friðland hafa og fá orlof af kongi, að hann halldi oss torg til matkaupa.'

Hjarrandi mællti: 'Vort torg skal yður til reiðu, en kongur bað mig til þín fara að segja yður, að hann býður yður til veizlu, ef þér vilið þiggja, um þrjár nætur, með svo marga menn sem þér vilið.'

'Það viljum vér gjarna þiggja,' segir Guðifreyr, 'og á morgin munum vér þar koma, eður er Hjarrandi kongsson í landi, er mjög er lofaður að hreysti sinni?'

'Að vísu er hann í landi,' segir Hjarrandi, 'því hann talar nú við yður.'

'Það er bæði,' segir Guðifreyr, 'að þú ert mjög lofaður, en þá lízt mér svo á þig, að mér þykir likligt, að það muni allt satt vera, sem vel er til þín talað, og gakk í vort tjalld og drekk með oss.'

Hjarrandi gjörir nú svo, og var þar af öngu drukkið utan gullkerum, og fannzt Hjarranda mikið um háttu þessara manna og alla atburði. En er honum þótti tími til, tók hann orlof til heimferðar og segir kongi, að þar var kominn kongsson af Galicía, 'og hyggjum vér, að þeir muni hafa eitthvert mikið erindi, þó að þeir hafi það eigi oss sagt, og koma þeir hér á morgin.'

Kongur spyrr, hversu honum lízt á þessa menn, en Hjarrandi segizt hvorki séð hafa vænna mann né kurteisara sveinafólk, og líður nú af náttin. En að morni kemur Guðifreyr kongsson heim til hallarinnar með sextigi manna, og voru þeir allir vænir og vel búnir. Hjarrandi gékk í móti þeim

---

[28] Along with *silki* 'silk', *pell* and *guðvefur* are two other distinct types of precious fabric. The three materials are often listed together.

kinds of woven silk and *pell* and *guðvefur*.²⁸ These men sailed to the harbour and carried tents onto the shore. The people thought it equally fashionable how they took in their sails as well as how a brilliant radiance came over when they erected their land-tents, because all directions were illuminated by the *carbunculus* set in the gold-wrought knobs standing on top of the tents.

Then the people tell the king that honourable men from a foreign land have arrived. He enquires about who they were, and sends Hjarrandi to the harbour. And when Hjarrandi arrived by the tents, many men came to meet him, and he saw one man there who far surpassed the others. Hjarrandi greets them courteously, and they him. He asks who their chieftain is. The handsome man said:

'I am called Guðifreyr, and I am the son of King Balldvini of Galicia.'

'We are curious,' says Hjarrandi, 'as to what errand you might have in our land, with such a large army.'

Guðifreyr says: 'We think it good to be prepared if someone wishes to deal us damage, but our large host will not bring you any harm, because we wish to find a haven here and receive permission from the king, so that he might have markets established for us to purchase food.'

Hjarrandi said: 'Our markets will be at your service, and the king asked me to come to tell you that he has invited you and as many men as you wish to a three-night feast, if you wish to accept.'

'We will gladly accept that,' says Guðifreyr, 'and we will come there tomorrow. Is Prince Hjarrandi, whose valour is much vaunted, in the land?'

'He's certainly in the land,' says Hjarrandi, 'because he's speaking with you now.'

Guðifreyr says: 'You are much praised, and it seems likely to me that everything that's said about you is true. Please come into our tent and drink with us.'

Hjarrandi does so. There were nothing but golden vessels to drink from, and Hjarrandi was greatly impressed by the conduct and manners of those men. And when he thought the time had come, he took leave for his journey home and tells the king that the prince of Galicia had arrived there, 'and we believe that they'll have a great errand, though they haven't spoken of it to us. They will come here tomorrow.'

The king asks how those men seem to him, and Hjarrandi says that he has seen neither a fairer man nor more courteous people. The night passes, and in the morning, Prince Guðifreyr comes to the hall with sixty men, who were all handsome and well-equipped. Hjarrandi went to meet them, and he leads them before the king. The king greets his guests well.

og leiðir þa fyrir kong, en kongur fagnar vel gestum sínum og sezt hann í hásæti sitt og Guðifreyr hjá honum, og margir ágætir menn sátu yfir kongsins borð. Hjarrandi sat á einum gylldum stóli, og það töluðu allir menn, að eigi hefði þar vænni maður komið en Guðifreyr. Drukku nú glaðir.

21. Kongur mællti þá til Guðifreys og spyrr hann að ætt og óðaljörð, eður hvert hann girntizt að fara, en Guðifreyr segir:

'Ég er son Balldvina kongs af Galicía, en af því að vér erum langt vestur í heiminn, þa lystir oss að kanna austurveginn og sjá siðu ókunnigra manna og kynnazt við höfðingja. Svo höfum vér og frétt, að þér eigið eina fagra dóttur, og forvitnar oss að sjá hana, ef það er eigi yður í móti eður hennar bróður. Svo höfum vér og spurð, að Hjarrandi, yðvar son, er íþróttamaður mikill, en við erum jafngamlir, en fjarstætt mun vera um íþróttir okkrar, en oss er sagt, að hans systur muni eigi gipt vera utan þeim manni, sem reynir íþróttir við hann, en oss þykir það skammlaust vera, þó að vér kómumzt eigi til jafns við þvílíkan mann.'

Hjarrandi mællti: 'Eigi ofhælið þér yður, en það eitt hefi ég um talað vegna Gullbrár, að ég mun því fram fylgja.'

'Gott þykir mér,' segir Guðifreyr, 'alla skemmtan við yður að eiga, hvort sem það eru skot eður skylmingar. Veit ég, að yðar systir er öngum góðum kostum að firr, hverjar íþróttir sem við prófum,[29] en eigi skulið þér svo virða, að mér gangi kapp eður ágirni til þessa.'

'Það skal vera,' segir Hjarrandi, 'en ég ætla vel fallið, að við prófum öðrum til skemmtanar okkrar íþróttir.'

Annan dag eptir geingu þeir á víðan völl, og var þá settur upp einn hár stjaki mjög. Þar setti Hjarrandi upp á eitt epli, og síðan tók hann sitt spjót, það sem þeir Vilmundur höfðu fyrr skotið. Hann skaut nú eplið ofan af stjakanum, og þótti öllum furða í því skoti. Nú er eplið upp aptur sett. Guðifreyr gékk þá til og setti eina hnettöflu upp á eplið[30] og gékk frá jafnlangt sem Hjarrandi og skaut á halann á hnettöflunni, svo að hún hraut ofan, en eplið stóð kyrrt og lofuðu allir þetta skot. Síðan prófuðu

---

[29] This is a complex sentence, literally meaning 'I know that your sister is no further from any good choices, whichever skills we compete in'. It was felt that its ambiguity would be more idiomatically expressed by translating the (dative) plural *kostum* as a singular noun. There seem to be two meanings of *kostur* at play here, in that it can mean (among other things) either 'a choice' or 'a good match for marriage'. In the former sense, Guðifreyr would simply be suggesting that any (good choice of) skill is ultimately equidistant from Gullbrá, that is, the challenge to win her remains the same regardless of which skills they compete in. In

He seats himself in his high-seat, with Guðifreyr beside him, and many excellent men sat at the king's table. Hjarrandi sat on a gilded chair, and everyone said that a man more promising than Guðifreyr had never come there. Then they drank merrily.

21. Then the king spoke to Guðifreyr and asks him about his family and native country, as well as where he was eager to travel. Guðifreyr says:

'I am the son of King Balldvini of Galicia, and because we live so far in the west, we desired to explore the east-way, to see the customs of unknown men and acquaint ourselves with their chieftains. Thus we received word that you have a fair daughter, and we are curious to see her—if neither her brother nor yourself object. We have also heard that your son Hjarrandi is a formidable man of skills, and though we are as old as he is, we are far off in our skills. We are told that his sister will not be married except to the man who competes in skills with him, but it seems that there would be no shame even if we could not prove to be the equal of such a man.'

Hjarrandi said: 'You aren't overpraising yourself—but I've only said about Gullbrá what I'm willing to follow through.'

'It seems proper to me,' says Guðifreyr, 'to share every entertainment with you, whether shooting or fencing. I know that your sister will be no further away from a good match, whichever skills we compete in,[29] but you mustn't assume that I would put special eagerness or ambition in those specifically.'

'Very well,' says Hjarrandi, 'and I think it would be proper for us to test our skills as an entertainment for others.'

The next day they went to a large field, and a very tall stake was set up. Hjarrandi placed an apple upon it. Afterwards he took his spear—the same one which he and Vilmundur had previously hurled—and he shot the apple down from the stake. Everyone thought that was a wonderful shot. Then the apple is set back up. Guðifreyr went to it and placed a *hnefatafl*-piece up on the apple.[30] He walked as far from it as Hjarrandi had, and he shot the tail-end of the chess-piece so that it fell down, but the apple stood still. Everyone praised that shot. Afterwards they competed in crossbow

---

the latter sense, Guðifreyr seems to be displaying characteristic false modesty in suggesting that their competition would put Gullbrá at no greater risk of landing a bad husband, whichever skills they contest, because he, Guðifreyr, would probably lose to Hjarrandi anyway (therefore implying that he would deserve her if he won). I am grateful to Dr Svanhildur Óskarsdóttir for her help in unravelling this passage.

[30] *Hnefatafl* is often simply translated as 'chess', as it was also a strategy game played with pieces on a board.

þeir arbystisskot og aðra hæfni, og var svo nærri um með þeim, að menn kunnu þar eigi mun að gera.

Nú kom njósnarmaður Vilmundar í móts við hann og segir honum, hversu geingið hafði með kongasonunum, og segizt öngvan mann slíkan séð hafa. Vilmundur bað hann fara enn og segja Hjarranda, að hann skylldi reyna allar íþróttir við hann Guðifrey utan berjazt.

En að morgni dags voru þeim búnir hestar til útreiðar með sæmiligum reiðskap, og þeir voru afburðar vel vopnaðir. Síðan tóku þeir stinnar burtsteingur og hlupu á sína hesta og ríða fram á völlinn. Hjarrandi kom fyrri á völlinn. Hann tók einn digran gullhring og rennir honum fram á götuna og hleypir síðan þar eptir hestinum sem harðazt getur hann. Og er hann kemur jafngegnt hringnum, stingur hann sínu spjóti í hringinn og kippir honum upp til sín, svo að hann seinkar eigi hestinn. Hringurinn loddi framan á spjótinu, en hann veifði spjótinu kringum sig. En þó hringurinn hryti af spjótinu, þá henti hann hann með spjótinu, svo að hann kom alldrei á jörð.

Nú kemur Guðifreyr á völlinn og hafði einn glerkálk í hendi, fullan af víni. Í annarri hendi hafði hann gullskál. Hann ríður sínum hesti sem mest mátti hann fara, en hans burstöng liggur í hans skjalldarhaka. Hesturinn rennur sem mest mátti hann, en Guðifreyr rennir á skálina, svo að hún var full, og ríður síðan að Hjarranda og réttir að honum og stöðvar eigi hestinn. Hjarrandi tók við skálinni og drakk af, en kastar hringnum til Guðifreys, en hann henti á lopti, og seinkaði hvorgi sinn hest og riðu til skeiðsenda og vendu snart um sínum hestum og hleyptuzt á móti, og afhendi þá hvor öðrum hringinn og skálina, og síðan leggur hvor í annars skjölld svo hart, að spjótskaftabrotin flugu langt yfir höfuð þeim, og skilldu þeir svo sitt turniment, og villdi kongur eigi, að þeir reyndi leingur.

Nú segir Hjarrandi sendimanni Vilmundar, að hann vill koma á sættum með þeim föður sínum, en sveinninn segir honum, að Vilmundur villdu það eigi, en hafði beðið hann að standa sér til, þá hann kæmi fyrir kong. Hjarrandi segir, að svo skyllldi vera. Síðan fara þeir til hallar, og prófuðu þeir nú skáktafl, og var um alla hluti nær um með þeim, svo að eingi kunni að mismuna, og geingur nú svo út veizlan.

En hinn síðazta dag veizlunnar beiðizt Guðifreyr að sjá kongsdóttur. Hjarrandi segizt það gera vilja fyrir vinskapar skulld, og var nú sent eptir henni, og var hún inn leidd með fögrum streingleikum. En þó áður væri bjart í höllunni og mikill ljómi, þá birtizt þó mikið, er hún kom inn, og síðan leitaði Guðifreyr þeirra mála við kong og Hjarranda, ef þeir villdu gipta honum jungfrúna. En Hjarrandi segir, shooting and other tests of marksmanship, and things were so even between them that the people couldn't tell any difference between them.

Then Vilmundur's spy came to meet him, and he tells him how things had gone between the princes, saying also that he had never seen such a man. Vilmundur told him to return and tell Hjarrandi that he should compete against Guðifreyr in all skills except combat.

The next morning, horses with proud harnesses were prepared for the princes for their tournament, and they were armed exceptionally well. Then they took strong lances, leapt on their horses and ride forward onto the field. Hjarrandi entered the field first. He took a thick golden ring and rolls it forth onto the path. Afterwards, he charges his horse towards it as fast as he can, and when he comes alongside the ring, he thrusts his spear through the ring and hoists it up to himself without slowing the horse. As the ring hung on the spear, he swung it around to himself, and even when the ring flew off the spear, he caught it again with his spear without it falling to the ground.

Now Guðifreyr enters the field. He had a glass goblet full of wine in one hand, and in the other he had a golden bowl. He rides his horse as quickly as he can, with his lance placed in his shield-hook. While the horse runs as quickly as it can, Guðifreyr pours wine into the bowl until it is full, and afterwards he charges towards Hjarrandi and stretches it out towards him, without slowing his horse. Hjarrandi grabbed the bowl and drank from it, while casting the ring towards Guðifreyr, who caught it in the air without slowing his horse along the way. They rode to the end of the course, turned their horses sharply, charged towards each other, and exchanged the ring and the bowl. Afterwards each strikes the other's shield so hard that the pieces of their spear-shafts flew far over their heads. Thus they ended their tournament, and the king did not want them to compete any longer.

Now Hjarrandi tells Vilmundur's messenger that he wishes to reconcile Vilmundur with his father, but the squire tells him that Vilmundur didn't want that, although he had requested him to stand by him when he came before the king. Hjarrandi says that he will do so. Afterwards the princes go to the hall, and then they competed in chess, and they were so even in all things that no one saw any difference. This continues throughout the feast.

On the last day of the feast, Guðifreyr asks if he can see the princess. Hjarrandi says that he was willing to allow that on account of their friendship, and she was sent for. She was led in to the sweet accompaniment of stringed instruments, and though the hall had already been bright and very radiant before, it was illuminated even more when she entered. Then Guðifreyr brought his suit before the king and Hjarrandi, asking if they would marry the young lady to him. Hjarrandi says that

að hennar vili skal fyrir ganga, en hún sagðizt það eigi á bak brjóta, sem þeir villdu.

Hjarrandi sendir nú mann til Vilmundar og spyrr, hvað honum þætti ráðligt hér um, en Vilmundur segir honum þætti það ráðligazt, að þessum manni væri eigi frá vísað, og segir, að Hjarrandi mundi eigi alla ævi hana geyma, og bað sveininn svo segja Hjarranda, að hann muni koma í brúðlaupið, hversu sem þeir kongur semdi, þá er þeir fyndizt.

22. Að morgni dags segir Guðifreyr, að hann vill vita sín erindislok og eigi eptir öngu þar að bíða. Geingu þeir nú í kastalann kongsdóttur og töluðu þetta mál við hana. En hún svaraði öllu hæverskliga, en segir þó, að henni þætti mikið fyrir að fara í ókunnugt land fjarri sínum frændum.

'Viljum vér og vita,' segir hún, 'hvað þér vilið fyrir vora skulld gjöra.'
'Hvers beiðizt þér, frú?' segir Guðifreyr.
'Oss er sagt,' kvað hún, 'að þér eigið eina systur, er Rikiza heitir, og ef þér vilið unna vorum bróður það ráð, þá þætti oss mikið gott í kaupazt.'

Kongsson svarar: 'Um öngvan hlut munu vér fortök hafa, en yðvar bróðir þykir oss sjálfur vera bezt til fallinn, að biðja þessar konu.'

Nú hvort sem hér eru um höfð mörg orð eður fá, þá verða þær endalyktir, að jungfrú Gullbrá var gipt Guðifrey kongssyni, og skal nú þegar vera þeirra brúðlaup, og var nú mikill viðurbúningur í borginni. Bauð kongur til sín vinum sínum og mörgu stórmenni, og var það mánuð heilan, að menn drifu úr öllum áttum að borginni. Það undruðuzt menn mjög, að Öskubuska ambátt var horfin, og vissi einginn, hvað af henni mundi orðið, og líður nú til þess, að komið er að brúðlaupsdegi, og skorti þá eigi allra handa hljóðfæri í höll kongs, og var höfðingjum skipað í sæti, og hafði Hjarrandi allt starf hér fyrir.

23. Nú skal þar til taka, að Vilmundur sat í kastalanum. Honum varð reikað burt í skóginn. Hann bað sína menn fara heim til borgarinnar og bíða sín þar, svo að eingi maður vissi, hvar þeir væri. En hann gékk á þá sömu sanda, sem fyrr höfum vér getið. Hann fer nú upp á steininn, og var hann þá læstur. Hann fór þá ofan af steininum og gékk þar að, sem honum þótti líkazt til, að dyrnar mundu vera, og lýstur á högg mikið og biður upp láta, ef nokkuð er kvikt inni, 'eður mun ég brjóta allan steininn.'

Nú var lokið upp steininum, og kom út kona nokkuð við alldur.

her wish must come first, but she said that she would not refuse what they wanted.

Now Hjarrandi sends a man to Vilmundur to ask him what he thought was advisable in this situation, and Vilmundur tells him that he thought it most advisable that this man shouldn't be denied, and that Hjarrandi would not be able to guard her for her entire life. He also instructed the squire to tell Hjarrandi that he would come to the wedding-feast, whether or not he and the king would get along when they met.

22. The next morning, Guðifreyr says that he wishes to know the outcome of his errand, without waiting any longer. They went to the princess's castle and discussed the suit with her. She responded very politely, but says that she thought it might be hard for her to go to a strange land, far from her kinsmen.

'We wish to know,' she says, 'what you will do for our sake.'

'What would you request for yourself, lady?' says Guðifreyr.

'We are told,' she said, 'that you have a sister called Rikiza. If you would grant her to our brother in marriage, then it would seem to us a very good agreement.'

The prince replies: 'We will not reject anything, but it seems to us that your brother is best suited to ask for the lady himself.'

Now, whether many or few words are spoken, things are concluded so that the young lady Gullbrá was married to Prince Guðifreyr. Their wedding feast is to happen immediately, and many preparations began in the city. The king invited his friends and many nobles, and for a whole month, people were coming from all directions to the city. The people greatly wondered at the fact that the bondwoman Öskubuska had vanished, and no one knew what had become of her. Time passes until the day of the wedding feast has arrived, and on the day there was no lack of all kinds of musical instruments in the king's hall. Chieftains were assigned to their seats, and Hjarrandi had seen to all the work.

23. Now the story is to be taken up where Vilmundur was sitting in his stronghold. He wandered away into the forest. He had told his men to go back to the city and wait for him there, without anyone knowing where they were. He went to the same sandy stretch that we have mentioned before. He climbs up onto the stone, but it was locked. He climbed down from the stone and walked to where he thought it most likely that the door would be. He strikes it with a mighty blow and asks that it be opened up, if anything is alive inside it, 'or I'll break the whole stone.'

Then the stone was opened, and an elderly woman came out.

'Hver ertu,' segir hún, 'er svo biður dyra?'

'Vilmundur heitir ég,' segir hann, 'eður hvað heitir þú?'

'Silven,' segir hun, 'ertu Vilmundur viðutan?'

'Kallaður hefi ég svo verið,' segir hann.

'Svo spyrzt mér til,' segir hún, 'að þú munir hafa unnið meiri hreystiverk en að brjóta stein minn.'

'Hvað er hér fleira?' segir hann.

'Vér erum hér þrjár,' segir hún, 'og á ég fyrir oss að ráda, og muntu láta oss vera sjálfráðar, ef vér lofum þér inn.'

'Vel mun oss saman koma,' kvað hann.

Þau ganga nú inn í steininn. Þær heilsa nú manninum, sem inni voru. Hann sezt niður og þótti þar gott um að litazt. Þær spyrja, hvað hann segir tíðinda. Hann mællti:

'Eigi þurfið þér mig tíðinda að spyrja, því að gjör vitið þér, hvað títt er í borginni, en ég.'

Silven svarar: 'Opt hefir þú vanið komur þínar á stein vorn, og ætla ég, að þú hafir hér flestra hluta vís orðið, þeirra sem þig hefir forvitnað.'

'Eptir er enn það eitt,' segir hann, 'sem mig forvitnar mest.'

'Hvað er það?' segir hún.

'Hvað að kvinnum eruð þér,' segir hann, 'eður því byggið þér hér?'

'Eigi skal þess dylja,' segir Silven, 'að þessi er mín dóttir, er hér stendur, en það er fósturdóttir mín, er á pallinum situr, og heitir Sóley, dóttir Vísivallds kongs.'

'Mjög eru menn þá duldir hins sanna,' segir Vilmundur, 'því að það hefir almæli verið nú langan tíma, að hún hafi verið hjá Kol kryppu í kastalanum og samþykzt hans ódæðum.'

'Því er betur, að það er ei,' segir Silven, 'en hún skipti litum við Öskubusku ambátt og hefir síðan haft hennar starf. Hefir hún og þess fundnar raunir, að þú gekkzt nærri henni einu sinni í steikarahúsinu.'

Hún tók þá upp eitt fingurgull og mællti til hans: 'Mantu, hvar þú skilldizt við þetta gull?'

'Þekkja mun ég þá hönd,' segir Vilmundur, 'og svo augun með.'

Þá lagði Silven fram hina hægri hönd fóstru sinnar, og sá hann þann fingrastað, sem holldið hafði hlaupið undan hans fingrum, og var nú þó hvítnað holdið um.

Vilmundur mællti: 'Bæði kenni ég gull þetta og hönd og svo augu, en þau sá ég hér fyrst í steininum, og það til marks um, að ég fann einn gullbúinn skó við þessa laug, sem hér er skammt í burt, eður minnizt þér nokkuð, jungfrú, þau orð, sem þér töluðuð, þá þér söknuðuð hans?'

'Who are you,' she says, 'who enquires thus at the door?'
'I'm called Vilmundur,' he says, 'and what are you called?'
'Silven,' she says. 'Are you Vilmundur viðutan?'
'I've been called that,' he says.
'Then I've heard,' she says, 'that you've accomplished far greater feats of valour than breaking my stone.'
'How many more are here?' he says.
'Three of us are here,' she says, 'and I'm in charge of us. If we let you in, you are to let us be free.'
'We'll get along fine,' he said.

Then they enter the stone, and the women inside greet the man. He sits himself down, and found his surroundings pleasant to behold. They ask what tidings he could tell. He said:

'You don't need to ask me for tidings, because you know better what's happened in the city than I do.'

Silven replies: 'You've been a frequent guest to our stone, and I think that you've gained knowledge here in most of the things that you were curious about.'

'One thing still remains,' he says, 'which I am most curious of all about.'
'What's that?' she says.
'What women are you,' he says, 'and why do you live here?'

Silven says: 'I won't withhold that. This is my daughter standing here, and that's my foster-daughter sitting on the step; she is called Sóley, the daughter of King Vísivalldur.'

'Then the truth has very much been hidden from people,' says Vilmundur, 'because for a long time now, it's been common knowledge that she's been with Kolur kryppa in the stronghold and approved of his crimes.'

'Fortunately that isn't so,' says Silven. 'She changed appearances with the bondwoman Öskubuska and has since taken up her work, and she has found proof that you came near her one time in the kitchen.'

She picked up a golden finger-ring and said to him: 'Do you remember where you parted from this golden ring?'

'I would recognise the hand, and the eyes as well,' says Vilmundur.

Then Silven laid forth the right hand of her foster-daughter, and he saw the imprints of his fingers where the flesh had been pressed and had now turned white.

Vilmundur said: 'I recognise both the golden ring and the hand, and also the eyes, but I saw them here in the stone first, and this is the proof: I found a gilded shoe by the spring a short way away from here. And, young lady, do you remember at all the words that you spoke when you found it was missing?'

Þá roðnaði Sóley, en Silven mællti: 'Eigi skalltu roðna, fóstra mín, því að eigi er víst, að þér bjóðizt vaskari maður. Hefir þú og það mællt, að þér þætti sú kona vel gipt, sem Vilmundur ætti.'

Hann mællti þá: 'Búið yður í stað, og skulum vér fara heim til hallar, og hefir kongur of leingi duldur verið hins sanna um dóttur sína.'

Silven segir hann ráða skylldu, og taka þær nú sína beztu gangvara og fara síðan heim til borgarinnar í þann tíma dags, sem Gullbrá var leidd í höllina með sinn skara. Menn Vilmundar kómu nú í móts við hann. En er menn voru niður setztir og til drykkju var tekið, kom Vilmundur í höllina og bar Sóleyju á handlegg sér, en þeir voru sextigi saman.

Vilmundur gékk fyrir kong. Hann mællti: 'Hygg að, kongur, hvort hér er komin Sóley dóttir þín eður hefir hún legið úti hjá Kol kryppu, sem þú hugðir, að vera mundi mágur þinn, en þá var þér viðurlíkur mágur makligur, og geym nú vel dóttur þina, en ég mun gjöra þér önga skapraun í hérvist minni fyrst að sinni. En svo finnuzt við næst, að þú verður var við, hvern þú hefir sekan gjört.' Snýr Vilmundr þá í burt mjög reiður.

24. Hjarrandi mællti þá til föður síns: 'Eigi er það vort ráð,' segir hann, 'að Vilmundur fari svo burt, að þið séð ósáttir, því hann mun verða þér sárbeitur í sektinni, en þú veizt það sjálfur, að vér villdum hann allir feigan fyrst, er hann kom til vor, en hann hefir oss líf gefið og í marga mannraun fyrir oss geingið og alldrei góð laun fyrir feingið af oss.'

'Hvað villtu þá til gjöra?' segir kongur.

'Þú skallt bjóða honum dóttur þína,' segir Hjarrandi, 'og þriðjung af Garðaríki og þá nafnbót, sem hann vill kjósa.'

'Valla er oss það lægingarlaust,' segir kongur.

'Eigi var honum minni smán gjör, þá hann var útlægur gjör, og hafði áður frelst þitt ríki,' kvað Hjarrandi.

'Far nú með sem þú villt,' segir kongur.

'Standið þér upp þá og fylgið mér,' segir Hjarrandi.

Kongr dvelur það ei, og hlupu nú allir upp, þeir sem inni voru, og geingu út með honum. Vilmundur var þá kominn á hest. Hjarrandi greip í taumana og mællti:

'Fyrir okkarn vinskap,' sagði hann, 'þá takið sættum við föður minn, því að hann vill bjóða þér góð boð.'

'Það gjöri ég fyrir þína skulld,' segir Vilmundur, 'en dauður skylldi hann nú, ef eigi nyti hann þín að.'

Þá mællti kongur: 'Vilmundur,' segir hann, 'far eigi burt, því vér viljum bæta það, sem vér höfum illa til þín gjört, með gulli og góðum gripum,

Then Sóley blushed, but Silven said: 'You mustn't blush, my foster-daughter, because it's not certain that you could be offered a more valiant man. You've said that you'd consider the woman whom Vilmundur married to be well wed.'

Then he said: 'Prepare yourself at once, and we'll go home to the hall. The truth about the king's daughter has been withheld from him for too long.'

Silven said that he would decide their course of action. They take their best palfreys and then go home to the city at the time of day when Gullbrá was being led into the hall with her train. Vilmundur's men then came to meet him. And when the people had settled down and begun drinking, Vilmundur came into the hall accompanied by his men, with Sóley on his arm; they numbered sixty in all.

Vilmundur walked before the king and said: 'Take a look, my king, at whether your daughter Sóley has arrived here, or whether she lay outside beside Kolur kryppa, whom you believed had become your son-in-law. He was then a fitting son-in-law for you. Now look after your daughter. I'll no longer cause you annoyance with my presence right now, but when we next meet, you'll know just who you've had outlawed.' Then Vilmundur turns away with great rage.

24. Hjarrandi then said to his father: 'It is not our advice that Vilmundur should depart with you two still unreconciled, because he will be destructive in his outlawry. You yourself know that we all wished him dead when he first arrived, but he has spared us and gone through many trials for us, and yet never received any proper reward from us.'

'What do you wish to do?' says the king.

'You must offer him your daughter in marriage,' says Hjarrandi, 'and a third of Garðaríki, along with whatever rank he wishes to have.'

'That would hardly be without disgrace for us,' says the king.

'It wasn't a smaller shame that was inflicted upon him when he was outlawed—and he had previously freed your kingdom,' said Hjarrandi.

'Let it happen as you wish then,' says the king.

'Then stand up and follow me,' says Hjarrandi.

The king does not hesitate, and everyone who was inside rose then and went outside with him. By then, Vilmundur had mounted his horse. Hjarrandi seized the reins and said:

'For the sake of our friendship, accept reconciliation from my father, because he wishes to extend you a good offer.'

'I'll do it for your sake,' says Vilmundur, 'but he would be dead now if not for you.'

Then the king said: 'Vilmundur, do not depart, because, for the evil things that we have done to you, we wish to compensate you with gold and fine treasures,

og þar til vil ég gefa þér mína dóttur Sóleyju og þriðjung af Garðaríki og þá nafnbót, sem þú villt sjálfur kjósa.'

Vilmundur svarar: 'Sóley er svo af konum, að mér er mest um, en Hjarrandi svo af karlmönnum, að ég mun flest allt fyrir gjöra, og því vil ég með hans samþyki þessi sætt taka.'

Sté Vilmundur þá af hestinum og var leiddur inn í höll, og var nú Sóley að þessum málum kölluð, og var þetta auðsótt við hana. Fastnar Vilmundur þá Sóleyju og fékk með henni þriðjung Garðaríkis og þar með hertuganafn, og skulu nú brúðlaupin vera bæði saman, og geingu þau fram með allmiklum skörungskap. En að afliðinni veizlunni voru allir með góðum gjöfum í burt leystir, og greiddi kongur út mund dætra sinna, og bjóst Guðifreyr heim í Galiciam, og var faðir hans dauður, er hann kom heim. Gjörðizt hann þá kongur yfir ríkinu. Vilmundur tók að sér það hertugadæmi, sem honum þótti gagnauðigazt í Garðaríki, og gjörði sér þar sterka borg. Hjarrandi dvalldizt með föður sínum nokkura stund, þar til að Vísivalldur kongur tók þá sótt, sem hann leiddi til bana. Hjarrandi lét gjöra sæmiliga útferð föður síns og bauð þar til Vilmundi mági sínum, og gékk sú veizla vel fram. Og að henni endaðri búa þeir ferð sína út í Galiciam, og sem Guðifreyr kongur veit það, þá fóru þau Gullbrá út af sinni borg meir en sextigi mílur og leiddi þá í borgina með miklum sóma og gjörðu þeim virðuliga veizlu, og sátu þeir þar allt það misseri, og var svo mikið vinfeingi þeirra, að einginn þóttizt við annan skilja mega.

En áður þeir fóru burt, gipti Guðifreyr kongur Hjarranda systur sína Rikizu, og tók hún í sína heimanfylgju það ríki, sem Gullbrá átti í Görðum austur, en Guðifreyr kongur tók þar í móti það ríki, sem Rikiza átti í Galicía. En að afliðinni veizlunni þá bjugguzt þeir Hjarrandi og Vilmundur heim í Garðaríki með mörgum stórum gersimum og ágætum gjöfum, er Guðifreyr kongur gaf þeim. En við þeirra skilnað var eingi svo harður karlmaður, að vatni mætti hallda, þeir sem á sá, hversu mjög við kómuzt þessir virktamenn og vinir í sínum skilnaði. Kómu þeir Vilmundur og Hjarrandi nú heim til sinna eigna og settuzt að sínum ríkjum og stýrðu þeim svo leingi sem þeim varð auðið að lifðu. Og endum vér svo sögu Vilmundar viðutan með því ályktarorði af þeim, sem skrifað hefir, að sá, sem lesið hefir, og hinir, sem til hafa hlýtt, og allir þeir, sem eigi eru svo ríkir, að þeir eigi kongi vorum skatt að gjallda, þá kyssi þeir á rassinn á Öskubusku, og takið það til yðar, allt slíkt sem hjá fór þá Kolur kryppa sarð hana, og sitið í þann frið, sem þér fáið af henni. *Valete.*

and furthermore, I wish to give you my daughter Sóley in marriage, as well as a third of Garðaríki and any rank that you wish to choose for yourself.'

Vilmundur replies: 'To me, Sóley is so exceptional among women, and Hjarrandi among men, that I will do absolutely everything for them, and I will accept this reconciliation with Hjarrandi's consent.'

Then Vilmundur dismounted his horse and was led into the hall. Sóley was asked about his suit, and it was agreeable to her. Vilmundur then pledges himself to Sóley and received a third of Garðaríki, as well as the rank of duke. The wedding-feasts were held together, and they proceeded with utmost honour. And at the conclusion of the feast, everyone was sent on their way with fine gifts, and the king paid out his daughter's dowry. Guðifreyr prepared himself to go home to Galicia, but his father had died when he returned, and he then became king over the realm. Vilmundur took for himself what he considered to be the wealthiest dukedom in Garðaríki and made a strong castle there for himself. Hjarrandi stayed with his father for some time, until King Vísivalldur succumbed to the illness that led to his death. Hjarrandi had a proper burial arranged for his father, and invited his brother-in-law Vilmundur, and the burial-feast proceeded honourably. When the feast had finished, they prepare for their journey to Galicia. As soon as King Guðifreyr learned of this, he and Gullbrá travelled more than sixty miles from his city, led them into the city with great honour, and arranged a splendid feast for them. They stayed there for the whole season, and their friendship was so strong that not one of them thought himself able to part with another.

Before they departed, Guðifreyr gave his sister Rikiza to King Hjarrandi in marriage, and she took as her dowry the realm east in Garðar which Gullbrá had owned, while King Guðifreyr took in return the realm that Rikiza had owned in Galicia. And at the end of the feast, Hjarrandi and Vilmundur prepared themselves to go home to Garðaríki with very many treasures and excellent gifts that King Guðifreyr gave them. And at their parting, no one was so hardy a man that he could hold back his tears, when he saw how much these paragons and friends were moved to tears at their parting. Then Vilmundur and Hjarrandi came home to their properties, and they settled down in their kingdoms and ruled them for as long as it was granted them to live. And so we end the saga of Vilmundur viðutan with this final word from him who has written it: that he who has read it out, and those who have listened to it, and all those who are not so rich that they have to pay tax to our king, can kiss Öskubuska on the arse: take for yourselves all that came when Kolur kryppa screwed her, and enjoy such friendship as you can get from her. *Valete* [Farewell].